Foreword

Oslo, May 2007: A seminar at the University of Oslo was held on organised crime. Amadeo Cottino, Paul Larsson, Petrus van Duyne and Klaus von Lampe held introductions, which were followed by an open discussion. In total, twenty researchers from Germany, Italy, the Netherlands, Sweden and Norway participated, all working within the fields of Criminology, Sociology and Law.

The main point of the seminar was the establishment of a presentation and discussion on organised crime in criminological and sociological perspectives. The seminar contributed to a discussion on both empirical findings and theoretical perspectives on organised crime.

In this anthology, we are happy to present the introductions from the seminar. We have also included an article by Per Ole Johansen, as well as one co-authored by the editors. Both articles highlight issues regarding organised crime that were discussed during the seminar.

Even though the articles presented are discussing organised crime in different arenas and on different analytical levels they have something in common. They all highlight some of the main issues currently discussed within the international academic debate on organised crime: What constitutes organised crime, how does organised crime work as a normative system, as a market and as an economic activity, how organised is organised crime, how international is it, how is organised crime regulated and controlled and what are the bases for these regulatory and controlling strategies?

In this regard we hope that students, researchers and others interested in organised crime will find the anthology relevant. We also believe that the different themes discussed in the articles should prove interesting to academics and others interested in crime, regulation and crime control in general.

Our approach is to present the article closest to one of the traditional approaches of organised crime, that is, a Mafioso way of acting, first and then go on to other empirical arenas and more theoretically oriented perspectives on organised crime. Thus, in accordance with our "readers manual', the most narrative perspective is presented first and the most theoretical approach, that is, the contribution that discusses organised crime on a meta-level comes last.

Articles are presented in the order of the following presentation of the authors and their contributions:

Amedeo Cottino; Sociologist and Professor in Criminology and Sociology of Law at the University of Turin, Italy. For a time in his career, he was the Cultural Attaché at the Italian Embassy in Stockholm, Sweden. He is currently working with economical crime in Italy.

In his article, he describes organised crime seen from within. Interviews with a former Mafia leader serve as a point of departure and he discusses organised crime as a normative system. How can we understand the normative basis of organised crime? One perspective is that the actions are supposed to serve the collective, that is, the family or the organisation. The dimension of "useful actions" is important when the Mafioso divides between actions and approaches that are acceptable or not.

Per Ole Johansen; Sociologist and Professor in Criminology at the Department of Criminology and Sociology of Law, University of Oslo; Chairperson of the Scandinavian Research Council for Criminology. His main research areas are economical and organised crime. In particular, he has published several books and articles on organised crime in Norway.

His contribution is a description of the Norwegian illegal alcohol market and a discussion about what happened with a market known internationally as Organized Crime Norwegian Style? After 2001, there was an unforeseen decline in the illegal alcohol market, a decline most commentators saw as temporary. Johansen asks what happened and what are we to expect from the "organised crime Norwegian style' in the future?

Paul Larsson; Criminologist and Professor at the Police Academy in Oslo. In recent years, he has held a variety of research and educational chairs within the police force. In his recent research, Larsson is predominantly focusing on policing and the regulation of organised crime.

His contribution is a current study of the Norwegian cannabis market. He discusses the cannabis market in light of statistics from, and interviews with, police and custom officers and also penal convictions. Critical questions under discussion are: What sort of business is the illegal cannabis market and how do we best understand and explain it as an economic activity? Who are the participants in this trade? How is this form of organized crime structured?

Vanja Lundgren Sørli and **Karsten Ingvaldsen**; both Criminologists and respectively holding positions as senior researcher and researcher at the Department of Criminology and Sociology of Law, University of Oslo. They are both active in research within the fields of organised crime and economical crime. Sørli is currently working on economical crimes in the taxi industry while Ingvaldsen is doing a research project on money laundering.

Their contribution is an article on organised crime in Norway since organised crime was introduced in the Norwegian penal code in 2003. How is organised crime conceptualised in Norway today, by lawmaking and convicting authorities as well as by newspapers? Which crimes does organised crime consist of? Who are convicted of organised crime and percepted to be organised criminals?

Petrus van Duyne; Psychologist and Professor of Empirical Law at the University of Tilburg, the Netherlands. He is Coordinator of the annual Cross-Border Crime Colloquium. In recent years, he has published several contributions related to organised crime, criminal business and cartel building, along with the organisation of crimes for profit.

In his article, he discusses "OCTA": Europol's Organised Crime Threat Assessment. Europol has developed their own annual enquete on which different organisations report their contact with organised crime. These reports form the basis for Europol's Organised Crime Threat Assessment. van Duyne discusses the methodology of the enquete and conclusions drawn by it and concludes that the Threat Assessment is built on an unstable foundation. The methodology and secrecy of the foundation of the concluding Threat Assessment form the basis for a discussion on up-keeping democratic rights.

Klaus von Lampe; Attorney and Assistant Professor at John Jay College of Criminal Justice, Department of Law, Police Science and Criminal Justice Administration in New York, USA. He is editor of the journal *Trends in Organized Crime*. Currently, his main research interests are strategic crime analysis, a follow-up of the EU-funded project, «Assessing Organised Crime», which was officially concluded at the end of 2006, and empirical manifestations of organized crime in two areas of crime: cigarette smuggling and drug trafficking.

His article consists of a description and discussion of the international research on organised crime. In recent years, the research on the arena has become more institutionalized; organised crime is now a research subject for governmental institutions both in need of, and producing analysis of, organised crime. Thus research on organised crime is entwined in political agendas with consequences pertaining to how organised crime is conceptualized, estimated and explained.

Neither this anthology, nor the preceding seminar would have been possible without the support and sponsorship of:
NSfK (The Scandinavian Research Council for Criminology).
Faculty of Law, University of Oslo.
Lovgivningsfondet, Faculty of Law, University of Oslo.
The Department of Criminology and Sociology of Law, University of Oslo.

Oslo, January 2009
Karsten Ingvaldsen   Vanja Lundgren Sørli

Innhold

How to regulate the evil: Organised crime and its norms
Amedeo Cottino 11

Organised crime Norwegian style ...used to be
Per Ole Johansen 41

Up in smoke! Hash smuggling the Norwegian way
Paul Larsson 63

Organised crime in Norway: An imported phenomenon?
Vanja Lundgren Sørli and Karsten O. F. Ingvaldsen 83

Searching the organised crime knowledge grail:
Disorganised EU threat methodology
Petrus C. van Duyne 119

The study of organised crime:
An assessment of the State of affairs
Klaus von Lampe 165

How to regulate the evil: Organised crime and its norms

Amedeo Cottino

It was a summer evening in Turin and Nino wanted to buy a slice of watermelon but the guy at the stand asked too much for it and said something like "if you don't want it, just go away". Nino left without saying anything. The following day however, Nino returned to the stand and shot the guy. Later, when I became more familiar with him, I thought on many occasions that I should ask Nino about the truth of this episode, which I was told by a magistrate of the Public Attorney office. I never dared to do it, however. In any case, this was the man I was going to meet in prison. His name was – and is – Antonino Saia, known as Nino, a former clan leader from Sicily found guilty of several murders, drug trafficking, extortions and so forth, who decided to collaborate with justice. Yes, I wanted to talk to an evil person, a person who had been practicing violence as though it were a normal, routine job. I thought, perhaps very naively, that should I succeed in winning his trust then I may find an answer to a very fundamental question: how can ordinary people do terrible things? This was an urge that went beyond the scientific curiosity to learn something more about the criminal world.

Thus, one day, I received a call from the Public Attorney office, informing me that Nino was willing to see me. I still remember the day: it was a Friday, quite early in the morning and I was nervously sitting in the attorney's car on the way to prison, unable to make any order of my emotions. I was nervous because I had never been in a prison before; I was nervous because I did not know how to approach him, how to tell him what I wanted to know. Actually, I was more than nervous: I was scared.

The room in which I sat waiting for Nino was a tiny, crude, shallow space with a table and two metal chairs. The door opened to a corridor where a guard was walking back and forth. I recall very little of this first encounter, except for a few things. I remember Nino entering the room with his handcuffs on (these were removed when he was seated), his impenetrable face and his eyes scrutinising me. I remember talking very fast, telling him who I was. I remember mentioning my children. I also remember telling him that I did not believe that there were good people and bad people, but just good and bad deeds. However, I know that I checked whether the guard was still there more than once.

Did Nino say anything himself? He most certainly did although I don't recall what he did say. For sure he agreed that we should meet again. This was the beginning of our story. We were two strangers walking the same path in search of a common humanity.

Thinking back, I believe that neither I – a fearful university professor – nor he – a cold-blooded, macho guy – realised how much our lives would become intertwined; how much we would end up depending on each other; how much my view of the world would change. For it did not take long until I felt that Nino was my guide, a sort of Marlow leading me down to the springs of evil. To put it in Conrad's words, "I was being made to comprehend the Inconceivable" (Conrad, 1999).

Even today, when many of those encounters come to mind, I can't help experiencing those emotions once more: a combination of stupor and horror. This is what I tried to express when I entitled one of the book's chapters[1] "The normality of evil".

What Nino was describing was not a "no man's land"; his landscape was not only full of corpses but of living creatures too. Although, unlike Dante's *Inferno*, the punishments inflicted were frequently lethal and were distributed according to laws unknown to me. However, I learned the laws; I learned them so well that, when tensions and fears started vanishing, I found myself to be truly sympathetic with Nino, many times. I was touched by his near pre-mordial attempts to search for explanations and meanings (the "why" of a forgotten childhood; the senselessness of a life nourished by death) and his honesty in acknowledging what was to me often inexplicable indifference vis-à-vis his victims[2].

---

[1] Our story resulted in a book (Cottino, 1998) where I related Nino's "rise and fall" as a professional criminal. Actually, he did not fall; rather he decided to quit his "job" and to turn to the Court. Thanks to his cooperation, dozens of his former comrades – and a few corrupt policemen, attorneys and judges as well – were tried and sentenced to jail. After fifteen years in prison, Nino is today at what the Italian law calls semi-liberty: he works outside the prison during the day, but must return to his cell at night. We see each other now and then and talk about work, children and sport. He is a normal human being.

[2] I realise that to speak of honesty in a criminal context is very much an oxymoron. Indeed, surely, in this specific case the reliability of the source represents a serious problem. Thus one could fear that Nino – aside from the perhaps inevitable distortions of memory – may have been influenced by the need to give himself the best possible image in his narration, in the hope of improving his living conditions, I am clearly unable, with

No doubt, my sympathy went very far, perhaps sometimes too far. I still remember that on one occasion, when Nino explained to me why a certain person had to die, my comment was: "Yes, I understand you". Many years have passed since that encounter took place and a profound unresolved uneasiness is still there. Did I really mean that, in his place, I would have killed a human being?

With the help of Nino's words, I will here illustrate how a criminal society is ruled and how the rules are applied[3]. First, however, let me give some glimpses into this man and his life. After all, he is the man who will introduce us into the Cursoti's criminal system.

Who is Nino?

The recurrent theme in the story of Nino is that of a double life:

---

any certainty, to exclude the possibility that he has assumed this attitude on occasion. Nevertheless, I am of the opinion that the distortions have not affected the essential parts of the story. I believe that I can make this affirmation upon the basis of a number of considerations. Throughout the entire course of our conversations, Nino demonstrated the desire not to hold anything back, not even the most odious parts of his criminal past and hehas blankly refused the role of a "victim of society". In addition, his version of the facts, compared to trial documentation where possible, has been confirmed. Furthermore, even his determined refusal to be anonymous may well indicate his strong desire to get to grips with his past. Finally, the material collected over a two-year period of weekly encounters shows a high degree of internal coherence. Incidentally, I should note that the third persons' names mentioned in the text are real names. They can all be found in the Turin Court official documents.

[3] I believe that criminal organisations like the Mafia, the Camorra and Nino's gang satisfy the criteria which constitute what can be called a legal system. The criteria are: the presence of a number of persons, a normative system and an organisation.

> Once you enter your house you forget what you leave outside (...) I would do a job and then we discussed it with my friends, my buddies. Then I went home and, for me, it was as if it did not exist (...) When one is with the family, it is as if you have lost your memory, of what you have done, of those particular things (...) I lived as if I was an ordinary office guy.

As our talks progress and we come to know each other better, the need for Nino to question himself regarding his past grows stronger. His childhood is profoundly marked by the imprisonment of his father, a fishmonger. The theft of a refrigerator costs his father some years of prison:

> I was very attached to my father (...) and I experienced it traumatically, in the sense that I closed myself up and perhaps it was then that (...) I don't know (...) Things started skidding for everyone and the family came apart.

What Nino recalls with no hesitation is the absence of a real childhood:

> I did not recall my childhood as nice. I never had tenderness from anyone. I'll tell you something: I never played in my whole life (...) I lived for the moment, stealing, bag snatching, and what I earned was mine.

Apparently, there were no economic restrictions in his childhood that negatively impacted on his future life. What he suggests instead is that the contact with people with previous criminal experience might have had a negative influence on him:

> I grew up on the street (...) I listened to the conversations of the others, to what they thought (...) All of these things which entered my head (...) and one grows. This is a culture. I always went around with people who were older than me, more criminal than me. Perhaps this had an influence.

In fact, Nino goes around with "bad company" very early. At fourteen he makes his first bag snatch, is arrested and spends some months in prison with adults:

> We were not in the same cell with adults, but we talked to each other. Twenty-two hours out of twenty-four hours shut in a cell: two sandwiches, two pieces of bread and some soup, at fourteen years old, for three and a half months. They did not allow us to listen to the radio, the newspaper was cut up; cigarettes (...) one packet per week!

Thus starts what can be called a "criminal career":

> As kids, all of us were petty thieves. Just about all of us did some crazy things. But that was inexperience (...) But, bit by bit, a guy would grow up a little and so he'd quit stealing cars, he wouldn't do that anymore,

instead he'd pull off a burglary, for example... of apartments. And finally he does a robbery.

Little by little, a gang is formed: a group of young people who call themselves the Cursoti[4]. Soon Nino's criminal talents place him in a leading position. Together with a few trustworthy comrades, he is sent to Turin[5] to control the drug market. These are years during which enormous amounts of money flow into the common fund[6] and Nino's share is one of the highest. However, this period comes to an end. Money, power and prestige can no longer hide his existential uneasiness. The time is ripe to experience what Hannah Arendt called the "wind of the thought" (Arendt 1978). He starts thinking:

> And already when a doubt arises in your head, you start to think that maybe that guy didn't have to die, but he was killed, and already this is a sign that you're starting to think about things. Perhaps in a way it could be a sign that you're tired of this life and also a sign of repentance, not in the sense of collaborating with justice but repentance inside yourself.

However, the difficulties to be overcome are enormous:

---

[4] The gang's name refers to one of Catania's central streets, Via del Corso.
[5] The industrial city situated in North-Western Italy.
[6] It was upon Nino's suggestion that the common fund was established. As we will see below, the fund was intended to cover expenses such as the lawyers' bills, economic support for the prisoners' families, the purchase of weapons and, of course, to distribute the dividends.

> Well, how many times did I, before going into action, feel really tired? Hey, sick and tired of everything, because I was doing what I was doing. There's the mental fatigue. Enough, I can't do it any more. How can I get out of this? A guy looks for some way out. This, though, is something you are saying inside yourself. Because a guy cannot, he can not say it, even to his very best friend!

Taking the decision to collaborate with justice is very difficult because its weight is different from each and every decision taken before, even the important ones. After all, Nino observes:

> Before doing an armed robbery, I'd already done some thefts (...) but it is very difficult to take the decision to betray your own companions. There is no comparison, really. Because with those people, a guy has lived so many years with them. Shared everything with them, you have even risked your lives together!

Nino recalls that the time after he had finally taken the decision to collaborate with justice as one of the most painful periods in his life.

> I felt like a worm (...) After a week, I wanted to die, truly. I wanted to kill myself (...) For a year, a year and a half, I was still asking myself whether I'd done the right thing (...) A guy thinks back about all that has happened over all these years, he thinks back about the people who are dead, either by my hand

> or by someone else's hand, and a guy, thinking it over again, says: hey, how was all of this possible? I mean, with these people, with a good part of them, we were all friends, we went out together to have a good time, many times and then, because of some choices, we were enemies. I was on one side and they were on the other side (…) I mean it doesn't make any sense at all (…).

Much more could be said about Nino. However, I will stop here, hoping that these selected biographical glimpses may give the reader a better grasp of Nino's life and character.

The rules

> How many times, for example, has the decision been made to eliminate someone, and how many times have I said: but hey, no. Back then, we had a rule that if one of us said no then all the others said no too because we didn't want any disagreement among ourselves. Either everyone is in favour or no-one. Why? Because common sense will tell you that, for a thing of that kind, it just isn't worth it.

As typically happens, in contexts and business sectors which are entirely legitimate heretoo, very important decisions, like whether or not to kill someone, can only be taken unanimously. The common sense to which Nino refers here is undeniable: the unanimity rule in decision-making reduces the risk of error by requiring a full airing of contrasting opinions before a decision is taken. Nino does not fail to underline the democratic nature of the decision-making process of the Cursoti, specifically contrasting it to the authoritarian style of the Mafia Families in general and the Santapaola clan – his sworn enemy – in particular:

> There were hundreds and hundreds of bosses, the ones who, sitting down, gave out the orders. With us, giving orders – it was all of us!
>
> There weren't some guys who said, 'You do this, you do that'. Yes, we did have a person who was Manfredi, who organised. He was an intelligent person, a person who had a number of friendships, who knew how to talk. We trusted him. But he was a symbolic boss, that is, in the sense that when the time came to take a decision, he first had to tell other people, that is, first he had to inform other people about his decisions. Instead, in the Santapaola group (...) it wasn't that way. If the boss took a decision, the others followed orders. These men[7] were people who said: 'Let's get our weapons and you guys get going'. They did this (...) and lots of other people like that.
>
> Then, when the war[8] turned really bloody, those guys escaped and they abandoned all those kids to their fate. Some went to Naples, some went to Palermo: they took their families and they went away, leaving those kids to be killed. That was the Mafia!

---

[7] The Santapaola clan's leader.
[8] Nino often uses military jargon to describe the recurring conflicts between the various criminal groups struggling for the control over the town of Catania.

> Because inside the Cosa Nostra, the group that makes the decisions never puts itself on the front line. They decide and then they delegate. One of these guys delegates and maybe I'm a soldier, I am a man of honour and a murder is assigned to me, I can't go to my boss or to the boss of the Family and say: Why do I have to kill that person? I am just a man of honour and I have to carry out the orders my boss gives me.
>
> But with us, it was never like that at all (...) That is, if we were all agreed and we'd talked about it and we gave someone the assignment to do the job, then it had to be done. That guy had to do it. Sure, logically, we'd see the people while we were talking about it and we would decide who to send and who not to send. Because there are always some people who have more ability than others. Maybe those others are more gifted in different areas, and, I repeat, we were always in the front ranks ourselves, even us, the guys who took the decisions.

It is this difference in the modus operandi on the part of the Cursoti which could result, in some cases, in the sparing of a life, as in the case of Pippo Tucci:

> One day they call us up: one of us has to go down there because there's a meeting since in the last peace treaty[9] it was decided that, when some person had to be hit, first you had to run this by the Family bosses.

---

[9] Between the Santapaola and other criminal groups.

If this person who had to be hit didn't belong to any of these Families, then the green light was given. If he did, you had to talk it over to explain the reasons. I go down to Catania: just about all of us were there (…) Anyhow, it was to talk about Pippo Tucci, the brother of Salvatore, to talk about the extortions he was doing, this guy was taking, I don't know, 150–200 million a year from a person. Besides that, they said he was an informer and that kind of thing so they wanted him dead. But it was mostly the Santapaola group (…) who really wanted him dead. While Pillera, the Pillera group were with the more moderate side. And so, at that moment, I'm the one who can tip the scales. Why was I the one? Because Salvatore Tucci, who was our guy in prison, was his brother and so I wouldn't go along[10]. And maybe in part it was the grudges and rancour between us and the Santapaola clan. So even if this Tucci had made a mistake, so as not to make the Santapaola guys happy, as we used to say, we told them no, even if later, on the quiet, we might later punish the guy.

So while everyone was there giving the thumbs down[11], that is, all the Santapaola group, I was the one who said no, we have to talk to him; and then, if he doesn't want to understand, action can be taken. But it has to be us who takes the action. You guys

---

[10] With the death sentence.
[11] An idiomatic expression meaning the death penalty.

must not try to take care of it yourselves over a thing like that.

Sometimes, in that type of situation, there are guys who, maybe to get noticed, to let their authority show among the men who are the most revered in the Santapaola clan, will just go along with proposals. This is wrong, since that way you are taking a human life when instead you could talk to him, at least try to persuade him not to do what he's doing. So going along with my counter-proposal, there's the Pillera group. But maybe if it was someone else (...). Next to me was a guy, Pippo Coppo, who said to me, no, this guy has to die and I said to him: you shut up; you shouldn't even let yourself speak up here. But Garozzo and Santapaola kept silent because at that moment I was the one representing the Family, it wasn't Garozzo anymore; if I wasn't there, it would have been Garrozzo who did the talking.

Another person, whose life was saved, in this case thanks to Roberto Miano, was Mimmo Inferera, a drug dealer. Even in the case of fair competition, according to the rules and in the name of control of the market, the established sanction was the death penalty:

> Around here, there was the policy that people who worked, either they quit working or they worked with us, or if not, they died. Especially those people who sold that garbage, those drugs. That powder was the most dangerous of all and a guy could cut that stuff in a lot of different ways. And this Mimmo Inferera

> was one of those kinds of guys who sell drugs even though he was a friend of Roberto Miano. And so, we sent word of this to Roberto Miano.
>
> Roberto, tell this person: 'Make a change! If you want to continue doing this work, do it in another city. But here, you'd better not sell any more of that garbage.'
>
> And so, Roberto told him and the guy went right on selling. And so, when we had sat down and we said, 'Hey, this guy is still selling, what should we do?' The decision to eliminate this person still had to be taken. Roberto Miano was against this (...) the guy was his friend. (...) Three of us were in favor and he was opposed. And so it wasn't done. It's an example about when you agree or disagree with the other people.

However, one should be able to express one's dissent. Giovanni Carnazza was killed by Salvatore Parisi when those who had opposed this murder had been sent to prison.

> Parisi came to talk to us three or four times about this killing: three or four times we sat down to talk and three or four times we said no, he didn't do anything. And then, as for us, they came and arrested all of us and only Parisi was left outside and so he did what he wanted. But before, when all of us were still outside, we didn't let there be any disagreement between ourselves, even if there was only one person who voted no.

> And so, sometimes, you had to think, hey, is what I am doing really the right thing? Like in that case, for example, you couldn't help but think, wasn't there some solution, couldn't we have gotten close to the guy?

The unanimity rule was not the only norm which prevailed within the Cursoti's operative scheme. Above all, as in the cases referred to above, a decision to be taken meant life or death for someone, the death sentence had to be preceded by a number of steps or measures, some of which display features common to popular culture. We might think, for example, of the prudence which is, as scholars have noted, a characteristic of the classic vendetta as practised in the interior areas of Sardinia[12].

> Before being killed, these people were called in, they were warned[13]: Forget about doing that thing you're doing or change the way you're doing that other thing. But extreme evils require extreme remedies. When there was really nothing else that could be done, then the guy was eliminated.

Thus, the universe of the Cursoti gang was not, by any means, a world without rules and therefore a world of total unpredictability.

---

[12] This profound difference manifests itself, for example, in the concept of *offense*, a behaviour which intentionally violates a norm of "the penal code". In this regard, see the reconstruction of the institution of the vendetta drawn up by A. Pigliaru (1995) and, in particular, the code of Barbagia, a very isolated province in the Sardinia island.

[13] The idea is to give the potential traitor or the unfair competitor on the criminal market a final chance to save his life.

In contrast to our own world, however, where there is a widespread ignorance about what our laws actually allow or forbid and where casual disobedience to too many rules is extremely common, within a criminal organisation everyone knows what is allowed and what is not. Consequently, deviance from established norms is (or has been, until recent times, due to the rapidly growing number of persons turning State collaborators) an extremely rare occurrence. This is not surprising when one considers that someone violating the norms of Nino's world is most probably putting his life at risk. As a result, a thorough knowledge of the rules of the criminal world is indispensable for anyone who wants to save his own skin. Fortunately, the number of norms that it is indispensable to know is rather small. There are, therefore, several analogies between Nino's world and ours, along with one very profound difference: the rules of the Cursoti gang and the effectiveness of those rules do not depend upon the so-called *fictio juris,* that is to say, the assumption (empirically, a rather fragile one) that the content of norms is known to those persons to whom those norms apply. The legal principle according to which "ignorance of the law is no excuse" is fundamentally extraneous to the criminal because in those worlds, ignorance of the law would be almost impossible .

Let us now list the main transgressions for which the death penalty is applied. Conceptually speaking, a person pays with his life for infringing upon either of the two fundamental moral goods imaginable: trust and honour (Cottino 1999). In contexts like that of many folk cultures, to which one may apply Foster's hypothesis (Foster 1965) that even immaterial goods may be seen as limited, the degree of conflict produced by the scarcity of these goods and by the competition to obtain them, is extremely high. Furthermore, it is by no means easy to exist without either of these goods. Trust, which is rather scarce within the larger social context, is clearly indispensable in the criminal world and crucial to the survival of the organisation. However, neither can one do without honour, since it lies at the interface between the private and the public sphere, between the image which the individual has of himself and the image others have of him. This conception, which to many of us might seem incomprehensible, has its roots in the archaic world, a moral universe even older than the "traditional" one. In the scheme of the archaic world, where the individual finds himself beset by an inescapable existential uncertainty, those very few certainties upon which he can depend are guaranteed to him by virtue of the recognition of his worth. This worth, an exclusively masculine attribute, is dependent upon possession of two kinds of property: land and/or animals and, in the Mediterranean world, women (Cottino 1993). This also explains why the costs of dishonour are so very high, as they do not only befall the man whose honour has been compromised, but also those who are connected to him. This explains the phenomenon, so frequently and dramatically reported in the media, of the family members of an informer rushing to denounce and distance themselves from their sons, husbands or brothers: they do so in order to preserve their own honour.

There are certain insults that are aimed directly at compromising a man's honour, for example, "cornuto", cuckold, and "sbirro" or cop:

> Because the cornuto has been betrayed by his family.
> Not by the criminal Family, but by his own family:
> his wife, mother, sister.

> And calling someone a sbirro means to accuse him of being a traitor. The sbirro is the one who drops the dime, who makes the phone call.

*

Then there is the azzampo:

> 'Azzampo' means that someone is ripping off his buddies. This is another serious thing. This is another very serious thing.

With these words, Nino introduces a story illustrating an episode of azzampo, or dipping in the pot. I recount this story verbatim below:

> The Miano brothers were the type of guys who always wanted to rip off everybody else. There was a time when Roberto Miano was the cashier of our group up here in Turin.
> And so, you know, each month, all the income, all the money coming in was divided up, and then there was money for the lawyers, for all the expenses. All the expenses were listed and all the monies coming in were written down as well.
> This azzampo, this dipping into the pot, was possible because there was such a flood of money streaming in and out. Like when I write 'general expenses, 100 million', I don't go and ask you what you bought with this 100 million. This is because every day you'd be buying weapons, every day you'd

be renting apartments for people, you'd be handing out money to friends. Every single day!

So you couldn't really check up on things. But, at a certain point, we realised what was going on. And that wasn't all: those Miano guys also worked, on the quiet, with other people. That is, behind our backs they worked with other people selling drugs.

And so when we first discovered this, we said we have to get rid of these other guys but Miano was opposed. And since we had that rule there, we said, 'Ok then'. Then one day I needed to have 50 million lire. We were looking to buy a bar in the Murazzi. We'd been talking to a guy about getting this bar there, renovating it completely and setting up in business. And it really turned out to be beautiful. And so, we agreed together and we said, all right, ok . And so, one day we had an appointment with that guy there.

And I said to him, 'I'll give you 50 million. You get started on the renovations'. And I'll take the brother of Franco Finocchiaro, Carmelo, and the nephew of Miano, Salvatore.

(...)

I say to them, 'You go in that house over there and you take 50 million'. I even said to them, 'In that house, just last night, we did the accounts and we left 86 million in cash'.

And they say to me: 'Are you sure?'

'Yeah, yeah, see what's written here? So you guys take that 50 million and take it to this other guy'.

And they say: 'Ok'.

After a couple of hours, they come back looking for me, they find me and they say, 'maybe somebody took it, like maybe Roberto (...) because he was the one who had the keys'. (Because back then, he was the one who kept the keys, was in charge of the cash box.) And these guys are saying: 'The money isn't there'.

And I say, 'Are you sure?'.

They say: 'There's, I don't know, maybe 10 or 15 million in there. Maybe it was Roberto who took it'.

Anyhow, 'Now I'll see', I say. 'I'll call Roberto Miano'.

He says: 'Hey, I didn't take that money'. Then he says: 'What 86 million? All that was left was about 15 million'.

I said that there were two other witnesses there.

'No', says Roberto, 'They are the ones who are wrong'.

And so, that's when we began to think (...) and then there were the drugs, the fact that he was selling on the side. We decided to eliminate Miano. As far as Francesco and Santo were concerned, people like that had to be eliminated. But, before we took him out, we talked to his brother Nuccio, who was in prison. We did that because he wasn't involved with this in any way.

So Franco Finocchiaro goes to the prison to see Nuccio, in Saluzzo I think it was, and he goes: 'You, this year, how much money have you taken?' We asked this because we were giving money to his wife. 'How much did you take?' And so the guy adds up. He says: 'I took such and such'. And it turns out that Roberto had dipped in the pot even on his own brother! He's ripping off his own brother! And here, we're not talking about 10–20 million, but hundreds of millions.

And so we say to him, 'Look, our accounts show this. There's no mistake because I took in so much, and the other guys have taken in such and such and so you must have brought in this other figure here'. It was then we decided to eliminate that person, all of us agreed: Parisi, Orazio, Giuffrida and Finocchiaro.

We decided. But, and I say it again, the same thing, the impression that Franco Finocchiaro was giving me, that somehow for a while he hadn't been the same, he'd been more nervy and wound up. And sure enough, then he informed the guys from Milan.

The Milanese guys came. The guy says, 'No, don't ruin everything. If there is something we have to pay, we'll pay it, maybe we can...'

'But what kind of talk is this? We don't want your money. This is something that belongs inside the Family!'

Anyhow, Franco Finocchiaro, maybe he talked to them, he'd thought twice about it: 'Hey, no, let it go anyway. Those guys', he said, 'they're pulling out'.

'What do you mean pulling out?' we asked.

(...)

> They deserved to die. On the basis of the code of honour of criminal society, they deserved to die. Instead, they got away with it because other people intervened and because those other people decided at the last moment to vote no. And Miano knew he was taking a risk, of course he knew! But that was 50 million all at one time, and there were plenty more too.

When Nino told him that he was taking the cash box away from him, saying: "Starting from today, you don't hold the cash anymore", Miano pretended not to understand the reasons why and he asked Nino to explain, Nino responded: "You're not holding it anymore. Someone else will do it. Maybe you're tired".

*

Then there's the traitor; the man who betrays his own comrades and thereby goes over to the enemy:

> There was another guy who was getting close to us and he was getting money from us in prison. And when he came out, he went with Nitto Santapaola. And so we lured him into a trap, it was in Milan: he was killed in a gambling parlour. With guys who break the rules, that's how it is.
>
> But not just in our group, in all the Families, in all the groups. Sure, when you're talking about a group of kids who go out to do robberies together, that

kind of thing, then these other things don't happen, because they don't have anything to divide up with other organisations.

Corrado Manfredi was killed because he was a traitor, although, within the context of the criminal organisation, it is almost impossible to be entirely sure that a betrayal has taken place. Actually, the person under suspicion will never be warned in advance by having specific charges brought against him; rather he will be judged guilty on the basis of circumstantial evidence. Corrado Manfredi was judged to have betrayed the trust of his comrades:

> An organisation can't just let these things go. If he hasn't betrayed us today, he'll betray us tomorrow.

*

Another serious infraction is molesting the woman of a comrade who is behind bars. Antonio Bulla, nicknamed "Nino 'u pazzu" or "Crazy Nino", was accused of having molested the wife of Filippo Cannavò – a courier for the Cursoti – and for this reason he was killed by Nino and Angelo Sciotti:

> And how was it that some people were dealt with? Sometimes, we dealt with someone because he had messed with the family of some guy in prison. This is what happened with Bulla, a kid, a guy around (...) One day I come for a prison visit. I ask for a prison visit to talk things over and I go off to find Francesco

Miano, who was in prison and there is Giuffrida with him.

Then Miano goes: 'Listen, you've got to see that it was Bulla who got them arrested'. There was Giuffrida and there was Filippo Cannavò. Young guys who were in with us. 'And beside this', he says, 'he molested the wife of this second guy'.

He says: 'You have to kill him'.

Was it true or wasn't it? I don't know. Maybe that guy has some personal quarrel with him, something like that happened before with others. Still, to eliminate these people who had never done anything to me, who never would do anything to me (...)

This was maybe the only murder I did as a hired killer. In the sense that the other guy wasn't a rival (...) I didn't even know him. Well, I kind of knew him (...) Maybe I'd seen him twice. He didn't interest me.

*

Finally, there's the bicycle or the tragedy. Turi Papale – erroneously believed to have extorted money from whorehouses in Catania, using Nino's name fraudulently – was wounded by Nino. While Nino himself admits that he was trying to kill him, fortunately Papale did not die. The two of them were protagonists in a situation called "the bicycle" or in more modern argot, "the tragedy". "To mount a bicycle" (or tragedy), in Nino's words, means:

> (...)that he's saying some things that aren't true (...) If I, for example, if I've got something against someone

or, if not, if I do something other people don't approve of, then I can say, 'But it was Joe Blow who told me to do this', that is, I get away with it myself because I say it was Joe Blow who told me to do it. So I'm doing a bicycle, this is a rotten thing, saying something about someone that isn't true.

Thus these are situations in which someone sets two other people against each other in order to clear his own name. This is reminiscent of a practice found in popular culture, as an example reported by Danilo Dolci attests:

> Let's say that I'm in a controversy with John Doe, then another guy, seeing that I'm at odds with him, this second guy takes advantage of the situation and kills me. Then everyone thinks it was John Doe and so he ends up in prison. The guy who takes advantage of an argument that way, they call him the tragedian.
> (Dolci 1960)

*

In the criminal society, there are also certain rules of conduct, which, although they imply sanctions in the event of their infringement, do not imply such radical sanctions as the death penalty. Still, they point to ways of behaviour that should be avoided. This is the case with the use of drugs and, in more general terms, with actions that are unjustified. Nino put it the following way:

Alcohol and drugs lead to mistakes. But not just within the Cursoti organization, they see things like that in all organisations. In an organisation, if there is someone who uses drugs, he's thrown out, because people like that are unreliable. If I take drugs, if I need to take drugs before I can go out and commit some crime, I'm unreliable because the day that I don't have that garbage, I'm going to do anything it takes to get some: I could even sell out to the enemy, I could even sell out to the police! And the same goes for alcohol.

How to understand the rules in a criminal society

Here the common points that I have mentioned, will be recalled and a few more will be added. How can we, based on Nino's words and other sources, understand the rules in a criminal society?

I: The criminal society too is founded upon the division of labour, both horizontally and vertically (there are robbers and extortionists, bosses and subordinates). It demonstrates a social stratification based upon "professionality" (one's criminal capabilities), income, and prestige (being a "named guy").

II: The criminals' business and professional activity, which presuppose a relationship of trust among the members, has profit as the driving motivation.

III: We are dealing with a group of people whose distribution of morality, should it be statistically shown along a curve, would prove to be normal. At the two extremes, the really bad guys – such as the brother of Nitto Santapaola, for example – and the good guys (men like Lanzafame, who sacrifices his life for his boss, or Salvatore Coppola, dedicated to helping others). Near the middle of the curve, we find the majority of individuals, persons who are neither very bad nor very good (to be clear on this: those who kill others only when they think there is no other choice).

IV: We are dealing with an organised society. Far from being prey to anarchy and disorder, it subjects its members to a highly strict and effective set of social control. This comes about through a system of rules which decree the illicit nature of a broad range of acts and behaviors, from the less serious, like the abuse of drugs or alcohol, to the most grave, like embezzlement from the organisation (*l'azzampo*). This long list of strictly enforced prohibitions is accompanied by a clear set of decision-making procedures (typically requiring unanimity), clear guidelines on salaries and profit distribution, and unmistakable procedures for the administration of justice.

However, social control is not exercised solely by law. The organisation has its own ethics, (distinct from Nino's individual ethics) shown, for example, in the refusal to live off the earnings of prostitution and in the respect for women and children. Nor is there a lack of social policies as assistance is provided to the families of prisoners, the prisoners themselves and friends.

V: The existence of an ideological superstructure which informs and regulates the administration of justice is related to this. To start with, the sanctions vary according to the kind of infraction involved. There's the death penalty, there's expulsion, there's the warning. But what is the ideology which underlies the use of the sanction? Is it, simply, the principle of retribution in its most archaic form – the so-called "eye-for-an-eye" – or do other ideologies underlie the punishments? In fact, we find the co-existence of a number of notions of punishment: from the retributive one (*"he deserved to die"*), to the idea of general deterrence (*"I wanted to make an example for the others"*), to that of special deterrence (*"a couple of good slaps"*). Resorting to technical language, we can say that the theories of punishment which inspire the Cursoti are not only those referred to as "absolute" – as is the assumption in a vendetta – but also those called "relative".

The principle of just desert is invoked in cases where the offence is serious: someone has played the informer, "the cop", or taken money out of the common cash box. Alternatively, they have illegitimately used the name of a respected person in order to achieve their own ends. In these cases, when the matters at stake are very high, say the trust or the interests of the organisation, the salvage of the individual no longer seems possible. Thus recourse to the death penalty – which is not automatic, as has been demonstrated in the case of Roberto Miano dipping into the cash box – is based on the logic of retribution: Joe Blow *deserved to die* because only the most extreme sanction is equivalent to the gravity of the damage that he has inflicted on the organisation. In other cases, capital punishment is justified by invoking the notion of general deterrence: the killing of John Doe will serve as a warning to others (as we can see in the case of Turi Papale). Clearly, both of these motivations can be implicit in the same decision. If, on the other hand, the offence is a minor one, the sanction – unlike the death penalty – is intended to have an individually preventive effect.

Perhaps my emphasis on the similarities between Nino's criminal society and our own can cause uneasiness: the uneasiness we tend to experience every time we enter into the "heart of darkness"; every time we are caught by the suspicion – or fear – that those who inhabit that world are not so different from us. This is not a good excuse to turn a blind eye, however. Nino, our guide, has led us over the edgewhich separates "us" from "him" and has that the criminal world is by no means a Hobbesian Leviathan, but a well regulated social system which, whether we want it or not, in many ways mirrors our own.

References

Arendt, H. 1978. *The Life of the Mind*. New York, Secker & Warburg

Conrad, J. 1999. *Heart of Darkness* [1902]. London, Penguin

Cottino, A. 1993. "Honor as property". *Journal of Legal Pluralism and Unofficial Law* 33, 4. 35–52

Cottino, A. 1998. *Vita da Clan*. Torino, EGA [French edition: 2001. *Vie de Clan*. Paris, L'Harmattan; Swedish edition, 2001. *Familjeliv – en maffialedare berättar*. Stockholm, Ordfront]

Cottino, A. 1999. "Sicilian cultures of violence : the interconnections between crime and local society". *Crime, Law and Society* 32, 2. 103–113

Dolci, D. 1960. *Documenti ed inchieste su alcuni aspetti dello spreco nella Sicilia occidentale*. Torino, Einaudi

Fiandaca, G. 1995. "La mafia come ordinamento giuridico : Utilità e limiti di un paradigma". *Foro Italiano*, V. 22–27

Foster, G. 1965. "Peasant Society and the Image of Limited Good". *American Anthropologist* 67. 293–315

Pigliaru, A. 1995. *La vendetta barbaricina*. Milano, Giuffrè

Organised crime Norwegian style ...used to be

Per Ole Johansen

The problem

The illegal Norwegian alcohol market, organised smuggling and illegal distilling, had its origin in the Prohibition, 1917–1927. For many years, the illegal alcohol market seemed to be an ever expanding market.

My professional interest in alcohol started over twenty years ago with a study of the Norwegian Prohibition, called *Brennevinskrigen* [*The War on Booze*]. My next book on the topic, *Markedet som ikke ville dø* [*The Market That Wouldn't Die*] was a comparative study of the Prohibitions in the USA and Norway (Johansen 1985, 1994). The follow ups, among them *Organized Crime Norwegian Style* and *The Come Back Boys of The Illegal Markets*, focused on contemporary markets (Johansen 2005, 2007). The titles gave a message about the adjustability and immortality of the markets. *Organized crime Norwegian style... used to be,* is a less convincing title. What happened then with a market that was internationally known as Organised Crime Norwegian Style?

The history of the market, from 1917 to 2001, is a story about talented criminal entrepreneurs and some very flexible and adjustable networks, in alliance with legal business. Prohibitions, rationing, very high prices and restricted availability were the preconditions for their economic success.

The first part of the article is about the good years, from the smugglers' and distillers' point of view, and an analysis of the reasons for their success. The next part focuses on the unforeseen decline of the illegal alcohol market after 2001, a decline most commentators saw as temporary, although they are not so sure any more. The import of methanol in 2001 and 22 dead customers killed the illegal market for 96% proof alcohol overnight. The extremely strong 96% was *the* illegal booze of the 1990s, imported in industrial quantities and mixed with coffee, or water and essences to be served as "vodka" and "gin". Illegal import of wine and beer, a local growth in illegal distilling, and a rather limited import of whisky and vodka and so forth have compensated to a degree, but fall far short of matching the *extent* of the market in the 1990s.

Increased police and customs' control or stiffer penalties are not the reasons for the decline. The control is actually currently at an all time low. The reasons are linked to the mechanisms of the market: lack of trust in the quality and safety of illegal alcohol, lower prices and better availability for legal alcohol, and new modes and attitudes, which are not economically *motivated*, but certainly economic in their consequences.

The history of the market

1917–1927: The Prohibition

The Norwegian ban on alcohol, from 1917 to 1924 for strong wines, and 1917 to 1927 for spirits, was originally a result of the First World War. Potatoes and corn were only to be used as a foodstuff, due to the limited supplies, warfare and blockades. The politicians in power felt a certain panic over hungry, angry and drunken workers in the big cities. A ban on alcohol was a guarantee of "social stability", they believed. Norway was neutral, yet it was influenced by the war in many ways. The Prohibition worked fairly well as long as the war was ongoing. The majority of Norwegians respected bans, restrictions and even a stronger State simply because of the war. Organised smuggling on the high seas was akin to suicide. Large-scale illegal distilling was impossible due to the lack of sugar.

The temperance movement, which was the biggest voluntary organization in Norway before the war, was eager to repeat the success of 1917–18, although this success was temporary and war-related. The police and the customs warned against a permanent national Prohibition; they were not prepared for such a challenge. The Norwegian coast was very long. There were only a few police and customs officers and they lacked modern equipment and intelligence systems.

The temperance movement got their way and *The New Day* was supposed to make Norway better, permanently so. They were right concerning change *as such*, for the next eighty years, but not the change that they had promised and hoped for. A huge black market for alcohol developed, from modest and "democratic" beginnings in 1917 to a professional market in the mid-1920s, with several sub-markets. Some of the markets had a life of their own; others interacted. Smuggling and illegal distilling were the main channels. A high level of organised smuggling meant a low level of illegal distilling and vice versa, although some districts "belonged" to smugglers *or* illegal distillers through the 1920s.

Doctor's booze was a huge market in its own right: legal prescriptions for any kind of "healthy" reason, for instance cold, fever, the Spanish influenza (not least), constipation, back pain, nerves, cold and rainy weather, painful menstruation, pneumonia, anorexia and so on. Friendly family doctors found it very hard to say no to patients they had known for many years. A minority of the doctors, a very active and cynical group, considered it to be "business as usual" and made fortunes by giving false prescriptions. Even "sick" animals got their alcohol. Norwegian dogs, cows and horses have never been as "ill" as in the 1920s.

Surrogates were the last resort for heavy drinkers, and the use of surrogates was at its highest in periods with few alternatives. Alcohol-based medicines, hair lotion, aftershave, mouthwash and even shoe polish were mixed and consumed, confirming the Norwegian proverb, "The Devil eats flies when he is hungry". Doctor's Booze and surrogates for personal consumption were Prohibition-specific and came to an end with the Repeal in 1927 – as sub markets.

There was a much larger American market in those years, due to the ban on *all* alcohol in the USA from 1919 to 1933. Norwegian business had a particular interest in the American market, although here we are referring to highly respected Norwegian shipping companies. Typical Norwegian smugglers, who lived by smuggling, did not have the infrastructure, the cover or the money for such a distance. Norwegian ship owners made fortunes in the 1920s by transporting vast quantities of liquor from European harbours to Rum Row on the East Coast of the USA, where American gangsters with speedboats took the booze for the last, risky stretch to the seashore.

Organised smuggling and illegal distilling for money survived – as subculture, as trade and market. That was a legacy of the

Prohibition. Another legacy was the very strict official policy on alcohol in the ensuing years. That latter kept the former alive for more than eighty years. Smugglers and illegal distillers saw the connection and were supporters of the temperance movement, some of them even gave money. High taxation of legal alcohol was their "bread and butter", they used to say. The politicians needed at least eighty years to see that connection.

1927–1939: Post-Prohibition

The illegal alcohol market did not disappear with the repeal in 1927. Indeed, it seemed to be very much alive in the years to come. The politicians believed legalizing spirits would undermine the "black market" demand, although they did impose some very heavy taxes on the newly legalized alcohol. Their naive optimism led them to ill advisedly reallocate some highly qualified anti-smuggling police units for other purposes. It took months or years to rebuild such valuable and specialised police competence, while the smugglers could re-establish *their* business in days or weeks. Breaks and restarts were a part of their lifestyle and modus operandi. The availability of legal alcohol in the 1930s was extremely restricted. There were only 13 state-licensed spirit and wine retailers in Norway, all of them south of Trondheim, hardly any of these were located in working class districts or the countryside! Legal spirit and wine stores in the 1930s were an urban, middle-class institution. Labour leaders were also temperance men, although for different reasons than those which their Christian temperance allies in the anti-alcohol crusade held.

Illegal distilling increased in the 1930s and proved almost impossible to contend with for over-worked sheriffs in counties where the majority of the population were protecting their local distillers. Sheriffs in "dry" counties had an easier job owing to temperance informers who kept a close and zealous eye on their neighbours; although that was no comfort for sheriffs in the *thirsty* counties. The sheriffs in the countryside were opportunistic, they had to be; they were in dire need of local goodwill.

The Commander of the Norwegian State Police declared "war" on the illegal distillers in a highly aggressive and optimistic manner, when he took over the force in 1931. In 1934 all of his illusions were dispelled. The combination of expensive legal spirits, local thirst and unemployed young men made illegal distilling a lucrative and tempting business. The only way to fight the problem, as the Commander saw it was by cutting the prices on legal alcohol – much to the irritation of the temperance movement. Illegal distilling, amateur and professional, had come to stay. Even big cities had illegal distilleries. Most distilleries were rather small, easy and cheap to rebuild following a seizure, nevertheless the *sum* of moonshine amounted to huge amounts when several thousand small distilleries were active all over the country for most of the year.

Illegal alcohol *smuggling* did not present much of a challenge for Norwegian smugglers either, due to the long coastline and excellent hiding places for illegal cargo. The Boys from the Prohibition were in their best years, and eager to stay in touch with their crime partners in Germany, Britain, Holland and the Baltic. Young American smugglers and gangsters who built a career on booze in the 1920s got at second chance after the Repeal in 1933 with *other* vices like gambling, drugs, prostitution, loan sharking and industrial "relations" (Haller 1985). There were no markets for those kinds of organised crimes in Norway in the 1930s, but illegal alcohol was still in great demand and continued to be the illegal money-maker par excellence.

The Germans were in the lead among the foreign smugglers in the 1930s, as it had been in the 1920s. Professional sailors, ex-officers from the First World War German navy and businessmen in Northern German harbours were the best smugglers and exporters. It was very tough for the coastguard and the customs officers in a low cost nation like Norway to keep up with them. The elite of the Norwegian smugglers were either professional smugglers or businessmen who combined smuggling and legal business, by using their legal infrastructure as a cover, for everything it was worth. Most of the company smugglers never touched the stuff and paid the East End Boys to take the blame in the court.

The beginning of the new war in Europe in the autumn of 1939 was the setting for the most peculiar rationing in the Norwegian alcohol history. The anticipated lack of petrol in Europe forced Norway to ration petrol. The Norwegian Wine and Spirits Monopoly decided to ration both the sale and transport of alcohol. The new rules allowed only four bottles of wine or spirits per purchase and just twenty-four bottles (no more and no less) for home deliveries per customer. Although it was a serious move, the Monopoly had no control over customers who visited several stores in one day or returned to the same store a few hours later. Customers who were used to four or five bottles for home delivery ordered twenty-four rather than none. The Government won both ways: the temperance movement won a symbolic concession, the Monopoly sold more than ever.

1940–1945: The Second World War

Germany invaded Norway in April 1940. *April 9th 1940* has been a traumatic date in the national psyche ever since. A great deal changed overnight: the military situation, politics, the economy, day-to-day life – even sales of alcohol. Professional smugglers knew they could not continue large-scale maritime smuggling with a new war on. Vessels lacking national identity and legitimate papers were maritime targets for everyone. *Abwehr*, the intelligence of the German Navy and the Norwegian State Police, kept a close eye on harbours and coastlines. Hitler thought the allies planned to invade Norway to start the liberation of Europe, the allies allowed him believe this.

The temperance movement recalled the First World War and made a predictable move. Corn and potatoes were in great demand, especially as the import of foodstuff was likely to decline. It would have been immoral to waste corn and potatoes on alcohol in such an extraordinary situation. The temperance people got their way, as did the Monopoly. A temporary ban on potatoes and corn for alcohol was understandable, but what about making spirits using sulphite, the Monopoly responded. Norway produced a large amount of chemical pulp for paper, of which sulphite was a component. It had to be separated in order to clean the paper and were thereafter thrown away. It was free, for several kinds of spirits, following an extra, albeit not too costly distilling. The temperance league could not match that. The Quisling regime wanted to please the Norwegians and capitulated.

The Monopoly got its way, albeit with a rationing system. However, "everything" was rationed during the Second World War: tobacco, foodstuff, clothes, shoes, all kinds of industrial deliveries and so on. The Norwegians had to apply for a ration card to buy a certain amount of wine and spirits a month. Most of them did; even temperance league men and women, so they could use the bottles as barter, to have more food, tobacco, clothes or whatever. The Monopoly produced and sold more spirits than ever. A lot of that spirit ended up in the "black" market where it was resold time and time again, for incredible sums. The black market of The Second World War was the mental and logistical link between the illegal alcohol markets of the 1930s and the post-war markets.

Moonshine was also made and sold on the black market, despite sugar rationing. Sugar quotas were resold and sugar was stolen from wholesalers and distributors. The German army was an important contributor, selling white sugar the "black" way. Money meant more than ideology. The State Police had no interest in fighting moonshine anymore. The Norwegian Resistance was its new enemy.

What about the professional smugglers from the 1930s and their co-workers in legal business, then? Many smugglers had to go the hard way, "social deprivation style" as petty salesmen in the black market – full time or part time. For legal business, the war was *business as usual* even more than ever. Many of *them* made fortunes by producing for and selling to the German occupying force.

Some smugglers did, however, enjoy a career more adventurous than simply selling bottles in dark alleys late at night. Professional smugglers had an interesting criminal capital. They were used to police, courts and prisons and knew how to read body language, remember faces and "smell" danger and informants. The organised smuggling of the 1930s was maritime. The smugglers remembered where to sail, to hide and where to land the cargo the safest way. Their pre-war networks were still partly intact too, among them German ex-smugglers who came to Norway in April 1940 as intelligence officers for *Abwehr*. The Germans did not waste time in calling their Norwegian contacts, to offer new jobs as informants, agent provocateurs or undercover agents on the west coast. Other smugglers were patriotic and joined the Norwegian resistance, while a handful played for both sides in the big "war game", cynical players, as ever.

1946–1959: Rebuilding

Norway lacked most things after the War. Industry, infrastructure, schools, the health system and private households had not been really regenerated since the 1930s. The years to come have been dubbed *The Great Rebuilding*. The German Occupation had changed a great deal, although not the politicians' belief in high taxation on alcohol. It was time for payback too, for the "liberal" alcohol policy of the Nazis. The post-war politicians started taxing alcohol the traditional way, this was in spite of warnings from the police who were very undermanned after the war.

The normalization of relations with Germany was a very hot topic for many Norwegians. The traditional interest in the German culture and language declined to almost zero. Angry Norwegians took to the streets in 1954 to demonstrate against the first German officers who were supposed to be stationed at the NATO headquarters outside Oslo. There were a few exceptions, however: a handful of Christians who believed in forgiveness, and pragmatic smugglers who believed more in money. The smugglers were among the first to renew their contacts with Germany, with legal shipping as cover in the first years and even vessels which sailed solely for the purposes of smuggling in the 1950s. German harbours and Norwegian fjords, which were known for smuggling in the 1920s and 1930s, were back in business.

Large-scale smuggling on the big passenger ships that sailed between foreign and Norwegian ports was a forgotten aspect of Norwegian alcohol history, before the veterans began to tell their stories. Young, up-and-coming smugglers, businessmen and chief stewards worked together over the years and made good money. Very few were caught for smuggling. Customs officers were partly bought off. The police had so much else on their mind, like the post war tribunals, which went on for years.

The 1950s marked the high point for illegal distilling, following the repeal of sugar rationing in 1952, just like it had been in the USA, in the 1950s. Distilling survived the war as a craft and subculture. Norwegian families had been used to taking whatever nature offered them and buying illegally ever since the war. The war experience scarred many of them mentally and rendered them life-long fixers with an eye out for a big opportunity. Moonshine was never seen as a crime, as long as the distillers kept a certain quality for themselves and did not sell to minors.

Several elderly Norwegian smugglers who I have interviewed over the years were freshmen in the 1950s. Veterans from the Prohibition served as their role models. The romantic nimbus of the Prohibition was very much alive in the collective memory. Like most memories, it was nostalgic and historically incorrect; nevertheless, it was a social reality and an inspiration. The freshmen from the 1950s carved life-long careers as smugglers and legal businessmen, at times, in a discreet and effective combination; splitting these two careers, at other times. They were big on networking and met a great many people from a great number of milieux and trades. The freshmen of the 1950s became the veterans of the 1990s – almost as eager as their predecessors. The oldest of them made his first deal in 1945, was first sentenced in 1947 and last in 2007 – just a few months before he died of natural causes. No police officers or customs officers have been in active service for so long. Who, then, represented tradition and continuity?

1960–1978: Tradition and modernity

The early 1960s to late 1970s represented both tradition and modernity for organised smuggling and illegal distilling. The society changed in many ways. When Norway started its *Swinging '60s*, the rebuilding was over. A new, liberal generation had its debut, asking for more booze than their hardworking parents. Norwegians went abroad for reasons other than business. Holidays in Spain and Greece, where alcohol was much cheaper, were becoming an alternative to traditional holidays in the hills and by the fjords. Norwegians travelled, imported and exported in *new* ways too. Civil airlines carried more and more passengers.

The Golden Years for the passenger ships on continental and overseas lines were to be history within just a few years. Smugglers who had made their living smuggling using these ships in the 1950s had to adjust, this they did quickly and accurately. Classical maritime smuggling had a certain renaissance. Smugglers with money invested in smaller but faster ships. Legal ship owners and fishermen tried their luck too. They knew how to sail a ship at least, unlike a new generation of city "gangsters" who were greedy, but without maritime experience whatsoever. Strange things happened in stormy weather out on the high seas.

The 1960s had something in common with the 1920s, such as party-life and maritime smuggling, but much more was different, for instance all the new articulated trucks which carried increasing amounts of cargo, legal as well as illegal. However, the smugglers did not complain, as the elderly custom officers did who were unfamiliar with the new infrastructure and rather frustrated. The customs officials knew the fjords, the piers and the ships. Trucks, roads and loading platforms were a new and confusing world. The smugglers had a head start, and knew how to use it. Wealthy smugglers bought their own trucks or paid drivers to smuggle for them. Alcohol was imported in a fairly organised manner in the years to come, camouflaged in the transport papers as "vegetables", "fruits", "furniture", "oil" and so on – sometimes transported together with legal cargo, sometimes alone.

Some drivers preferred to smuggle for themselves. They never imported huge quantities, which could have cost them a great deal in the event of seizure, merely around a hundred bottles, or less when they were otherwise on the road for legal business – nevertheless it proved to be a nice tax-free income in the long run. The police were more eager to catch "the big fish" and so let the small ones swim through.

Illegal distilling changed in the 1970s. Distilling became more common, even in the cities Technological improvements and high quality products in modern distilleries were the new trends.

1978–1986: Four liquor strikes in nine years

1978 to 1986 was a period partly characterised by business as usual with traditional distilling and smuggling, but it was extraordinary too, with four "spirits strikes" in nine years. The relationship between the leadership of the Monopoly and their workers was not at its best. The leadership was old fashioned and easily offended. The strikes were both a question of wages and were a result of bad relations. The union leader was well mannered in private settings, but was aggressive and very radical when it came to wages and union rights. The leadership could not stand the union leader, who was not an easy personality to get on with. The Monopoly wanted to get rid of him and did not try to hide it.

The huge illegal market of the 1990s was supposedly a result of the four strikes from 1978 to 1986, but history is seldom that simple. The illegal alcohol market was established many years earlier. The veteran smugglers from the 1950s, the sailors from the 1960s, the drivers from the 1970s and a group of updated distillers were already in business, eager to meet the new demand when the workers went on strike.

However, the strikes ushered in a big change in other ways: the smugglers became accustomed to handling bigger quantities in a shorter time, and formed links with new groups of customers. Logistics were also greatly improved. The distillers had to meet an endless demand, which freed them up to make moonshine that was either high quality or just good enough to be a happy medium. No-one could meet the new demand alone. A new generation of independent entrepreneurs, who otherwise would have been working for the big shots, got their chance. Similar to the American Prohibition in a manner, big city gangsters now had interests in booze, but could not meet the demand alone. They could see no reason then to block the youngsters who saw the chance of a lifetime and grabbed it (Haller 1985).

The Norwegian press was a part of the markets in the 1980s too – in a way – by informing their readers about the dramatic lack of legal booze, that smuggling and moonshine were blooming and discussing how to order alcohol from abroad. The lack of legal alcohol caused national hysteria for some, a "moral panic" never before seen in modern times.

1987–2000: High season

So many success stories about smuggling are never told. That's partly why they *became* a success: the discretion of the entrepreneur. However, three teams from the 1980s which kept going into the 1990s – with a certain change of modus operandi – are known.

I have met them and got their story. They were quite successful, despite being caught after a while. They made big money for years before their downfall and knew how to reinvest or spend the money before they had to do time, or were *supposed* to do their time. One of them met an understanding doctor who claimed his patient was too sick for prison. The others did their time as model prisoners and used the period for further education, in legal or illegal business. Two of the teams were big in spirits from Germany and Holland. The third team imported 96% pure alcohol from Spain, for years – pioneer style.

Spirits such as vodka and whisky were the dominant items for Norwegian smugglers in the 1970s and 1980s. The very strong 96% proof alcohol from Spain represented the future and was an omen for the incredible success stories of the 1990s. The Spanish distillers could barely believe what they saw: Norwegian trucks picking up industrial quantities of 96% every week for the Norwegians to *drink*. The 1990s were "the great years of the 96", while spirits such as whisky, vodka, gin and so forth lost their traditional dominance in the illegal market. Beer and wine were small submarkets for amateurs and part-timers, which professional smugglers regarded with contempt.

The *early* 1990s, however, were not that easy for professional smugglers. A new generation of police investigators and customs officers started to cooperate. This was something new; previously the police and the customs had been rather competitive and mutually suspicious of each other, since almost the Second World War. The new team were young and "hungry" and knew how to recruit informers from smugglers and distillers. The smugglers knew that the police and customs "knew", but never exactly what and how they knew. The police and the customs got the upper hand for a while. Some smugglers became paranoid and switched to cigarette smuggling, applied for social security or took a break. The more experienced began to split up the cargo before crossing the borders to make themselves less "professional". They knew that time was on their side. "Wars" against organised crime never last for long. The police have so much else to do and politicians tend to interfere.

It is very important to bear the difference between police rhetoric and police practice in mind when it comes "wars" against organised crime. Some police commanders played "the organised crime card" when applying for the subsequent year's budget, rather like police unions negotiating for higher wages. They were simply tactical, like all professions. Most police officers were never in touch with organised crime, even less so with alcohol smuggling. About five officers in Oslo specialised in fighting alcohol smuggling and illegal distilling in the early 1990s. They remained a team up until around 1993 and were quite professional, albeit a very small team compared to the anti-drug department of the Oslo Police, which had about 100 men and women. Nevertheless, even five specialists on illegal booze may have been too many, for some higher up. The team were assigned other orders.

The rest of the 1990s were *on – off* for the police and high season for the smugglers. The smuggling of alcohol in the 1990s was like a huge river where everybody could fish: veterans from the 1950s, sailors from the 1960s, drivers from the 1970s, freshmen from the liquor strikes and a brave new generation with its debut in the 1990s. Amateurs, part-timers or professionals; there seemed to be sport along that river for everybody, until the import of methanol in 2002, that is.

2001–2007: The methanol and beyond

The import of methanol from Portugal in 2001 and 22 dead customers killed the market for 96% pure alcohol in a single blow. Smuggling lost its innocence. It was no longer a case of "crimes without a victim". The smugglers did not intend to import methanol, which was meant for industrial purposes and highly dangerous for people to drink. Why should the smugglers ruin their own business? Why the distillers in Portugal exported methanol instead of pure alcohol is still unclear. It could have been due to an accident: someone tried cynically to get rid of an overflow of methanol, or someone wanted "pay back" for unknown reasons – according to different informants. Only the distillers in Portugal know the answer and the sources there are not very reliable.

The Norwegian smugglers felt the heat as they never had before, when the police investigated the methanol. Methanol and dying costumers was clearly something other than pure, classical smuggling. One of the biggest investigations in Norwegian crime history made being a smuggler very unpleasant and it was highly stigmatised. The menthol was front-page-news for months. The importers became public enemies and the bandits of the year. Names and pictures in the newspapers, broadcast live on the television channels direct from the courtrooms; no anonymity whatsoever!

Commentators as well as smugglers were confused about the future of the illegal market. Some thought it dead and buried forever; others saw the recovery as a question of time, owing to the big thirst and the short memory of the customer. The answer seemed to be rather complicated, and still is.

The market for 96% proof alcohol is almost dead, with a few local exceptions. Ever since the methanol incident, the illegal import and distribution of wine and beer has been both very big and organised to an extent that it has never been before. The organised smuggling of beer and wine was on the road at a pace that stunned everybody. Wine and beer is imported from Germany, not from Spain and Portugal as the 96% was, Transport is a question of mere hours. Smart smugglers import smaller cargoes more often, rather than risking the large, "professional" loads. Smugglers who live along the border between Norway and Sweden, where more of them have settled down in recent years for practical reasons, know where it is safe to cross and when. New networks and teams, unknown to the police and the customs, came into their own. Beer and wine is even seen as more "moral" than the 96%.

The illegal market has survived due to a radical readjustment. It is not to be underestimated. The "milieu" has a long-standing tradition for creative entrepreneurship, but the market is *not what it used to be*. It is a new and interesting market out there, but it is not huge as it was with 96% pure alcohol in the 1990s or spirits in the 1980s. It is still organised crime – at least an illegal market, but it is not *Organised Crime Norwegian Style* anymore. Instead it is just an illegal market among other illegal markets at the present time. Norwegians are still thirsty, so how can that be?

Success and stagnation

The long success story of illegal alcohol in Norway is a consequence of the official alcohol policy and a huge demand for alcohol, which never seems to be satisfied. Very few saw smuggling and illegal distilling as real crime.

The most successful smugglers have been very flexible. They knew how to adjust, and the best time for expansions or breaks. Changing networks were more effective than so called criminal organizations. Routines would have made their business predictable and risky. Sudden growth was bad for business too, because size meant visibility. Technological innovations were used to confuse the police and the customs. No bragging; no large sums of money in the open; no mistresses; no paper trails; information on a "need to know" basis; counter-surveillance. Partners and families helped when the main operators were in prison. Violence was the very last resort, should it be used at all. The smugglers sought alliances with legal business, or started legal companies to cover the import and have ready answers should the taxman started asking questions. They discussed which answers to give the police if asked in advance, and made a show of good manners when they did meet the police, customs or the judge. They were model prisoners while doing time, telling themselves about the new possibilities around the corner, even while they were locked up.

Just as professional smugglers have done for almost three generations, the freshmen learned from the veterans. Episodes became experience. Experience turned into collective criminal capital and tradition. Yet smuggling has still declined, in spite of all those Best Practices. It is still a market in its own right, but it has not been modest for many years. This is despite the control of the police and the customs being at an all time low. Why could this be so?

Quality and safety

Most customers lost their trust in the 96%, due to the methanol incident. The accompanying media and deaths have kept that fear alive. There may even be more risky stuff out there, left over from the import in 2001. The customers have seen a disaster unfold and think it may happen again.

The romantic nimbus of the good old days is gone. The smugglers have lost their prestige; they are no longer seen as harmless. Survivors among the victims asked why did they had not seen the danger coming? The methanol tragedy was traumatic for the smugglers too when they encountered grieving families in the courts. Some of the smugglers could barely hold back tears.

Prices and service

The leaders of the Norwegian Wine and Spirits Monopoly have "always" been willing to fight smuggling by cutting their own prices, but the politicians have been very much against this. A few years ago, something started to happen. For one reason or another, the real prices for spirits seen in relation to the consumer price index were reduced 20% from 1998 to 2004. The nominal price level for spirits declined by more than 30% compared to the index for nominal wages and salaries. It is almost a historic cut, for Norway. The number of licensed wine and spirit stores skyrocketed to around two hundred in the late 1990s – while there were thirteen in the 1930s. Visiting a licensed spirits store in the old days approached punishment with poor service and arrogant or ignorant attitudes, the customers often had to wait in line while a suspicious police officer kept his eye on them. Today one is met by professional service and staff members who know what they are selling and are happy to give advice. There is either self-service or you can go to the information desk, according to personal preference. The only police officers to be seen in the stores are those who are there to buy alcohol themselves.

Modes and status

The generations who went through the Second World War and the Great Rebuilding were fixers with an eye out for the big opportunity, proud of knowing their way around. Moonshine and 96% pure alcohol, fresh from Spain, mixed with coffee or a tasty essence made the guests happy and the host proud. Arrangements like that seem strange and odd for most of us today. It is unthinkable and would have been next to scandalous in urban, trend-setting milieus, while illegal distilling was pretty common some years ago, even among leaders in private business with exams from the top universities. The host of today is supposed to offer high quality alcohol, wine or spirits. Buying cheap and illegally, or making your own booze gives no prestige, with the exception of certain districts with a strong cultural identity in moonshine. High quality, tax-fee spirits are the only "cheap" urban exception today, indeed how can the guests know?

Neither the veterans, nor the new generation of smugglers are dumb. They have both guts and talent, but they have just met market forces stronger them themselves.

No hope for the future?

To quote an amusing Norwegian proverb, it is hard to make predictions, especially about the future. At least when it comes to the peculiar alcohol culture of the Norwegians, I would like to add, but let's try anyway. Open borders and an increased flow of people and gangs travelling around may lead to an increase in organised crime, according to a common belief. This may be so for certain crimes and vices, such as theft followed by instant "export" or prostitution, but not for the more advanced, professional smuggling. Closed borders have – on the contrary – been triggering professional smuggling. Professionals have done what amateurs could not do, or lacked the guts to do. Open borders or a lower level of control along the borders afford the amateurs and part-timers their opportunity. *That* is the lesson of the European history of smuggling from the 16th century to the present time.

References

Haller, M. 1985. "Bootleggers and Businessmen : From city slums to city builders". Kyvig, D. ed.: *Law, Alcohol and Order : Perspectives on National Prohibition.* Westport. CT, Greenwood Press

Johansen, P.O. 1985. *Brennevinskrigen.* Oslo, Gyldendahl

Johansen, P.O. 1994. *Markedet som ikke ville dø.* Oslo, Rusmiddeldirektoratet

Johansen, P.O. 1996. *Nettverk i gråsonen : Et perspektiv på organisert kriminalitet.* Ad Notam, Gyldendal

Johansen, P.O. 2004. *Den illegale spriten : Fra forbudstid til polstreik.* Oslo, Unipub

Johansen, P.O. 2005. "Organized Crime, Norwegian Style". Duyne, P.C. van, K. von Lampe, M. van Dijck & J.L. Newell eds.: *The Organized Crime Economy : Managing crime markets in Europe.* Nijmegen, Wolf Legal Publishers

Johansen, P.O. 2007. "The Come Back Boys of the Illegal Markets". Duyne, P.C. van, A. Maljevic, M. van Dijck, K. von Lampe, & J. Harvey eds.: *Crime Business and Crime Money in Europe.* Nijmegen, Wolf Legal Publishers

Weding, L. 2007. "Organizational patterns for large-scale alcohol smuggling and alcohol distribution in Sweden : A pilot study". NSFK: *Hva kan de som ikke vi kan? Om Vinnere i organisert kriminalitet og økonomisk kriminalitet.* Oslo, Nordisk Samarbeidsråd for Kriminologi

Up in smoke! Hash smuggling the Norwegian way[1]

Paul Larsson

Trafficking of hash has, until recently, been an under-researched field in Norway. This is mainly because the interest, and research-money, has preferentially gone to studies of heroin and other more sexy and potent drugs. The few studies conducted on hash have mainly been local studies of drug pushers (Sandberg & Pedersen 2006) and the smaller trading networks (Smith-Solbakken & Tungland 1997).

Since our knowledge concerning the trafficking of hash is limited, my goal is quite simply to map what is known about this topic in Norway. In contrast to researchers that view hash as a trivial and common drug, and hence of little interest, I adopt the opposite stance. It is interesting that a drug that is viewed as commonplace and used by a substantial stratum of the population is nevertheless criminalised and penalised to a considerable extent in

---

[1] I extend my thanks to the moviemakers Cheech and Chong, for the title "Up in smoke".

Norway. The ESPAD reports[2] documents that Norway, along with Sweden and Finland, are the European countries with the lowest cannabis usage and experimentation. However, the consumption of hash still reaches a few tonnes per annum[3]. The combination of the fairly harsh degree of criminalisation with widespread acceptance of use in large segments of the population is enough to, by itself, trigger the interest of any criminologist.

In this article, I will present some findings concerning hash trafficking as a form of illegal trade. What sort of business is this and how do we best understand and explain it as economic activity? How is this form of organised crime structured? The question of who becomes involved in this trade is also raised. In international literature, different types of smugglers are presented (Adler 1993, Desroches 2005, Junninen 2006). Are these entrepreneurs best understood as businessmen, hedonists or adventurers?

My study is based on an analysis of 34 court cases concerning smuggling of large quantities of hash (15 of these were trafficking shipments of more than 100 kilograms), on police and custom officer interviews, on police intelligence and reports produced by these agencies and other open sources such as yearbooks and official statistics. The data can be said to be rather one sided, there is scarce information from the smugglers themselves. Treated critically, my information provides some valuable data on *where, who* and *what* to build the analysis on. My research doesn't pretend to

---

[2] ESPAD publishes an annual report on alcohol and drug use among students in 35 European Countries. This is known as the ESPAD report.
[3] Guesstimates of the consumption are fairly flexibile, yet a figure of 5 to 15 tonnes a year is plausible, when the known user population and their consumption is then matched with seizures (Larsson 2006).

give a "true" picture of the trafficking of hash, rather that which can be documented from official sources.

My aim has been to understand how hash trafficking is achieved, how the trade is structured and who gets into this business. Some might ask: "Why study these aspects? We know they are in it for the money". The simple answer is that money can't explain it all. If profit was their only interest, they could have chosen another trade such as cigarette or alcohol smuggling, one more economically rewarding, less risky and with shorter penalties (Johansen 2004). The rational *economic man* would presumably start in the trade of wine and beer smuggling to Norway (Larsson 2008b).

Trafficking in hash

When I started, my original aim was to map the trafficking of *cannabis* to Norway. I soon found that the import of marijuana, with a few exceptions, is minimal: the seizure figures are typically several tens of kilograms per year. This is a clear indication that marijuana consumed in Norway is usually produced here. The open market for marijuana is minimal or nearly non-existent, most is sold within networks of friends. Marijuana cultivation in attics, yards or greenhouses has, in most cases, been rather small-scale, amateurish and for local consumption. The professional cultivation by Vietnamese networks that has been uncovered in rental houses is a new form of the industry[4]. Thus far, 41 plantations have been

---

[4] It bears similarities with the production in the Netherlands described by Duyne and Levi (2005). In Norway, we have a long tradition of bootleg liquor production that dates back at least a century. There may well be some similarities between this and marijuana production (Johansen 2004).

found in Norway. One might well wonder, which market all this hemp is intended for.

Trafficking in hash is not a new trade. The interest in regulating this activity became apparent by the end of the 1960s and the early '70s. It appears as though the various forms of smuggling have developed in much the same way in Norway as in the UK, according to the description of the latter by Dorn, Murji and South (Dorn, Murji & South 1992). Thus from more ideologically oriented trading charities and mutual societies in the 1960s and '70s to bigger more profit-oriented activity. However, the greatest proportion and resulting actual figures of smugglers apprehended is typically small-scale: they bring home small quantities for personal consumption and that of their friends and neighbours.

When we examine the seizure figures, we get a different picture: one that predominantly reflects the resources invested in the regulation of trafficking by customs and the police. This might indirectly tell us something about the volume of smuggling. The focus upon drugs and the resources put into "the war on drugs" escalated from the mid 1980s onwards. Use and possession of even small quantities of hash was criminalised in 1972 (Christie & Bruun 1985). An increase in political pressure upon the war on drugs and resources resulted in ever-rising numbers of drug convictions and seizures during the 1990s. In 1980, 6% of all penal reactions were against drug related crimes; in 1994, the number had increased to 19%; and, in 2006, to 40%.

This development has changed somewhat over the last few years. The former minister of justice ordered the police to cut back on chasing "small fry" and to concentrate on serious big volume traders and traffickers instead. The result was a drop in small cases from 2003 – 2004, especially in Oslo, and an increase in larger cases. This trend has since been reversed due to political pressure, so now the figures for less serious drug offences are on the increase once more.

Hash seizures

As a point of departure, a curious fact: the price of hash sold on the streets has been constant for over 30 years. It has been, and is, 100 kroner or £10 a portion, approximately 0.7 grams.

Seizures of cannabis by the police and customs. (Amounts are in kilograms. Source: National Police Directorate)
- 1990:   230
- 1995:   19 900
- 1996:   711
- 1999:   1 254
- 2001:   881
- 2002:   1 230
- 2003:   2 300
- 2004:   2 200
- 2005:   1 324 (of these, 28.5 kg marijuana was spread over 140 seizures.)

The extreme number of 1995 can be explained by one seizure, of a little over 19 tonnes of marijuana, from a Colombian ship headed for the Netherlands. The numbers of seizures have also risen.

Numbers of seizures by the police and customs:
- 1990: 4274
- 1995: 4941
- 1996: 4296
- 1999: 8485

Since the turn of the millennium, there have been around 10,000 seizures a year. This tells us that the average seizure size is small; in 1990, the average was 54 grams, while, in 2004, it was 220 grams. The increase in kilograms can be explained by a few notable large seizures. This is confirmed by a number of big cases involving 300, 400 and 500 kilograms of hash over the last decade, whereas such seizures were extremely rare prior to 1995. Whether this is an indication of the smuggling of bigger loads or improved results of the police and customs is not yet clear. There seems to be evidence to support both recent trends of bigger loads and also increased police resources and developments in investigative techniques, notably the surveillance of mobile phones and deployment of intelligence, yielding better results.

Analysis of seizures by the police shows that most of the hash sold in Norway is produced in Morocco[5]. The route to Norway goes via Morocco, Spain, then onto the Netherlands and later to Norway. Most of the hash confiscated in Norway has been smuggled directly from the Netherlands or Spain, although some has been bought in Denmark (Copenhagen). Norway has an extremely long cost-line with many fjords and small islands but most of the seizures are made at the border to Sweden, in Svinesund, where the highway from Denmark (the E6) crosses the border. There are also

---

[5] The figure 80% is often mentioned here.

seizures at the ports, mainly on ferries from Denmark, all along the South coast of Norway. There are some obvious holes in customs control, typically relating to smaller ships and vessels that are in such numbers that they prove very hard to control. Most of the hash smuggled into Norway is brought through Oslo en route to destinations around the country. Intelligence shows that the route typically passes through central, eastern Norway.

The trafficking of hash as a trade

Organised crime is often seen as predominantly a profit-oriented activity (van Duyne 1993; 2006). Economic perspectives and motives are therefore typically deployed in order to explain smuggling and other forms of organised crime. The smuggler is transformed into an economic actor, rational in their manners. In this way, the market perspective is introduced into the analysis. We now speak of legal and illegal markets, drug markets, heroin and hash markets, cigarettes and alcohol and so forth. The study of how they are organised and structured, how the money flows and the different roles of the players in these markets have afforded us valuable knowledge about how organised crime operates in the Nordic countries (Johansen 2004; 2005, Skinnari, Vesterhav & Korsell 2007, Vesterhav, Skinnari & Korsell 2007, Larsson 2006; 2008). These studies go a long way in documenting Paolis' argument that the majority of such markets are "disorganised" and share a number of distinctive traits, as they are markets in *illegal* goods and services (Paolis 2002). Organised crime markets are indeed different from legal and open markets in many respects.

The drug markets have, in particular, been described as highly profitable. The hash market alone is often said to be overflowing with easy money. Confiscations and seizures of drugs are always presented by the street value and calculations built on these measures show that a great deal of money ends up in the pockets of the traffickers. This logic is similar to the concept of a Volvo-dealer being able to put the entire sale amount in their own pocket, each time they sell a car. The many hands it has gone through, the taxes levied, the shipping of the car and all the other expenses the car has to cover is forgotten.

A calculation based on known prices[6] at different levels can give us an idea of the profitability of hash trafficking to Norway. In this example, we shall use 100 kilograms of hash to simplify the calculation. The price in the Netherlands equates to approximately 1,500,000 Norwegian kroner (roughly 150,000 pounds sterling) – with variation according to quality and quantity. Although cash is king, part of this sum will be on credit, depending on whether the customer is trusted or a new buyer. If the hash is sold in gross, in Norway, the price can be as low as 20,000 kroner per kilogram: 2,000,000 Norwegian kroner (200,000 pounds sterling) for 100 kilograms.

We can therefore see that the smuggling team can make around 500,000 Norwegian kroner (a little under 50,000 pounds sterling) on 100 kilograms bought in the Netherlands[7]. However, the shipping costs on drugs can be substantial. One of the court cases reveals information about Danish truckers that were paid 1 million kroner to smuggle 500 kilograms – a sum that seems reliable

---

[6] The prices are gathered from information by police and customs, much of this is confirmed in case-papers.

[7] The Netherlands is the preferred country for buying medium and slightly bigger bulks of hash. When it comes to more substantial shipments, Spain is used quite often. Smaller scale trafficking goes from Denmark to Norway in many instances.

as there is other information that verifies it. Accordingly, we can allow for another 200,000 Norwegian kroner (18,000 pounds sterling) if professionals are used. In this case, the smuggling team would be left with 300,000 Norwegian kroner (once 200,000 kroner has been deducted from 500,000 kroner). However, there are other expenses to account for also. Smugglers are usually big consumers, they use mobile phones extensively, live in hotels, eat out and have a lifestyle that soon diminishes any profit. If they use drugs themselves, parts of the shipment often disappear as there are normally a few "good friends" hanging around to help consume it. It certainly costs to live as a criminal. We must also consider that the money is split between helpers.

There are many risks connected to trafficking, one of which is bad hash, another is that helpers "eat off the shipment"; the stuff can be seized by customs and the police and unreliable assistants can also steal the goods[8]. On top of this, there may be problems getting money from the customers, a substantial part of the sale is on credit. There are also costs in connection with moving cash to the Netherlands in order to pay off the supplier[9]. With a few clear exceptions, the rule often seems to be: the more you examine the drug economy, the more the big money evaporates before your eyes. In order to make a substantial profit then one has to smuggle in bulk, volumes amounting to hundreds of kilograms. In Norway, few have the capability, knowledge, cash and contacts to do so. Norway is a rather transparent country, with a rather limited

---

[8] In one of the cases, there was an account of a "helper" that absconded to Spain with 420 kilograms of hash; such instances are bound to be damaging.
[9] This can be achieved in many ways, although it is not unusual to use specialized curriers.

number of known organised criminals and this renders large-scale smuggling risky (POD 2005). Not everyone has the possibility to become a successful entrepreneur in this business (Adler 1993).

In many instances, it might be best to operate on a small scale. When hash is available at 20 – 25,000 Norwegian kroner a kilogram in Norway and the price in Denmark is 17,000 Danish kroner; one might wonder why some are willing to take on the risk and trouble of a trip to Denmark in order to buy small quantities. The answer could be that they don't have contacts in Norway who supply hash at a low price. In Denmark, it is available on the street[10]. The low Norwegian gross prices indicate that these sellers are either near the importers or that they more or less buy directly from the traffickers. Either way, it may well be profitable to smuggle a kilogram to friends, even if it is sold cheaply and the smuggler consumes part of the load of it personally. There is a great deal to indicate that these *entrepreneurs* exclusively supply themselves, friends and acquaintances. In many ways, this appears to be a separate market, where the smugglers rarely move into big-time trafficking. They resemble what has been described as "mutual societies" (Dorn, Murji & South 1992): these are networks of friends that help each other out by supplying drugs.

The larger scale smugglers in my material are typically what can be called criminal diversifiers, who are known to be active in different criminal activities. For some, the hash business is fairly central, while to others it is one of many forms of criminal activities. In my material, I have also found examples of what has

---

[10] Christiania in Copenhagen used to be an open market. Indeed, the main street is named Pusher Street.

been described as opportunistic irregulars[11] (Dorn, Murji and South 1992). These are persons who are not usually involved in crime, they smuggle drugs because the opportunity arose and they were tempted by the possibility of making fast money[12]. Quite a few of the drug couriers seem to be of this type.

Hash trafficking as informal economic activity

If we take the social relations and studies economic activity as a form of social exchange to be a starting point for our analysis of organised crime, we get a somewhat different picture than that which is usually presented. Typically, the actors are seen as rational, profit-maximizing atomistic actors. The drug markets is often described as a form of cottage industry (Eck and Gersch 2000). They are small scale and often fairly "home grown", rather than large and streamlined. Johansen documents that those who survive in the trade of alcohol smuggling are characterised by small, flexible arrangements (Johansen 2004). Trafficking of hash to Norway shares the same features (Larsson 2006). The same can also be seen, in studies of the Swedish drug markets (Vesterhav et al. 2007).

It was via anthropologic studies of so-called primitive economies that researchers discovered that many societies had a substantial volume of economic activity that was not registered in the Gross

---

[11] Dorn, Murji and South (1992) describe seven different forms of trafficking "firms". These are trading charities, mutual societies, criminal diversifiers, opportunistic irregulars, retail specialists and state-sponsored traders.
[12] Desroches (2005) also describes these in his book. They are often "white" businessmen in financial trouble that, in some way, have contacts with organised criminals, often from the same family or ethnic background.

National Product (GNP). This was frequently only a rather small fraction of that which was registered and known. They also found that, quite often, production and sale was not on the open markets, instead that economic exchange was often tied to networks involving friends and kin.

> Goods and services did not have to be produced and consumed in officially recognized and registered enterprises. Instead they could be made, traded, swapped, and bartered among members of informal networks.
> (Ferman, Henry & Hoyman 1987, 10)

Goods were traded and redistributed in many different ways, not only by the use of money. This was, and is, an efficient means of doing "business" because the trade was made between acquaintances with pre-existing social relationships: economic activity was merely one aspect of much broader social activity. Economic activity is thus social in character.

> Informal activity that takes place largely in personal and intimate social domains will often offer gratifications different from any material rewards that may also be obtained and these gratifications will be of equal or greater importance.
> (Gaughan & Ferman 1987, 16)

Studies of the former Soviet Union and Eastern bloc countries yielded much the same findings. A secondary economy had developed on the side of the known official economy. There were markets for goods and services that were otherwise hard to attain or illegal on the open market. Networks selling and distributing these goods were established, often called black markets. In these one could get everything from toilet paper to Western commodities.

Later on, studies of "developed" Western economies also had much the same findings: a broad spectrum of informal economic activity, both legal and illegal. A broad range of studies over the few last decades has focused on black labour, although this is just one type of informal economic activity; other examples include smuggling and trade in drugs, alcohol or cigarettes (Schneider & Enste 2003).

We are not going to dwell on the scale of the hidden economy; instead we will examine the qualitative aspects of these activities. The informal economy has some characteristics that are often pointed out, these are as follows:

- The importance of the social relationships and networks.
- Economic activity is a form of social exchange.
- Markets are dominated by a range of non-economic norms and values (and these have cultural traits).
- Money or profit is not normally the most important goal.

Nearly all types of economic activity are forms of social interaction. There are sound reasons why the illegal economy is, to a high degree, centred around networks of friends and close relations. It is easier to control the spread and flow of information in such groups. An effective way to ensure the control of information leakages is by working with people you know very well and are sure that you can trust. You need to trust that your collaborators won't run away with the goods, the money or cheat you in other ways. We often find such alliances this within ethnic groups; one reason to account for this is that we trust our own:

> ... there is a tendency among groups to define members of one's own race and/or ethnicity as trustworthy and view others as outsiders.
>
> (Desroches 2005, 46)

An important finding from research on organised crime in the Nordic countries over the last decade is that criminal groups typically take the form of networks. These networks vary in flexibility and density but most of them are distinguished by the fact that members know each other well and have grown up together. In this way, the distinction between what is labelled criminal youth gangs and organised crime groups is often quite hard to discern. The difference most often found is that the organised crime groups have, to a large extent, progressed to carrying out systematic crime in order to gain profit (Larsson 2008a).

Businessmen, hedonists and adventurers

There are two questions that we have not yet asked: Who are the traffickers, and what are their motivations?

Fredrick Desroches differentiates between two types of traffickers: one is the businessman who lives an otherwise rather law-abiding life and who typically has a background in legal business, the other is the "criminal" dealer (Desroches 2005). The businessmen describe themselves as entrepreneurs and are highly ambitious, hard working opportunists. In the majority of cases, they are not drug users themselves and tend to be non-violent. The "criminal" dealers are embroiled in criminal careers and lifestyles, they typically have a rap sheet featuring prison sentences, in many instances for quite serious crimes. Two-thirds of Desroches' informants who were incarcerated for drug trafficking had been successful in legal business before they became involved in drug smuggling. They were motivated by the possibility of making fast money in smuggling and also the thrill and the adventure.

Mika Junninen describes his informants; Finnish organised criminals, mainly traffickers, as professional criminals and adventurers (Junninen 2006). The term professional criminal was developed by Sutherland (1937) and describes a person that has chosen crime as a profession and means of making a living. The criminal has a professional attitude towards crime, doesn't commit crime when drunk or intoxicated and their acts can't be explained as symptomatic of psychological reactions or revenge on society (Junninen 2006). Instead, the professionals are fairly rational actors, competent and capable in what they are doing. Hawkeye Gross' handbook in smuggling gives a first-hand view into the world of the professional criminal (Gross 1992). Gross describes the partners recruited for smuggling adventures as follows:

- They should have combat experience (so that they tackle stress well).
- They should not abuse alcohol or drugs.
- They should be unmarried, without children.
- They should not be "tricksters" – people who will attempt "smart" things such as stealing or using counterfeit money when buying drugs.

The smuggling trade requires the learning of techniques to avoid getting caught and to develop a career. The requirements are many and the checklist long. Gross, along with others that have studied drug smugglers, points out that in order to be successful smugglers must appreciate the challenges and the thrills; the money is not *the* most important thing, but the lifestyle (Gross 1992).

The professional criminal and the businessman do not share many similarities with the traditional criminal as described in mainstream criminology[13]. However, they do resemble many types of white-collar criminals, often described as relatively rational and well off (Larsson 2002).

A problem with these generalisations is that we may find what we are looking for. Studies of organised crime have underlined that much of the crime is short-sighted: led by the quest for pleasure and gain. There is an "easy come easy go" logic where the opportunity of making quick money and scoring drugs is often followed by both the money and drugs being consumed straight away (Adler 1993, Van Duyne 1993). "Easy come, easy go" and "life in the fast lane" are seen as the most central elements in this way of life. Consumption of drugs and money builds status. Eventual economic remainders are invested in trades and businesses that the smugglers know and trust (such as car firms, pubs and apartments), although, most commonly, it is channelled into other criminal activity.

Nevertheless, it is also possible that all of these varieties of being and acting can be found. Traffickers might (like most people) be complex individuals, who seek adventure, act as professionals and who also like to party. Adler (1993) seems to support this view, while the majority of Desroches' (2005) businessmen did not use drugs and were more motivated by the money. It is possible that a professionalization has occurred between the time of Adler's fieldwork on the US West coast in the 1970s and the Canadian traffickers of

---

[13] At least in Nordic criminology, that still predominantly focuses on blue-collar crimes.

today for example. The size of the markets should have an effect on the trade. There is no place for giants in the limited market of the relatively transparent and well-mapped underworld of organised crime in Norway. Small size and flexibility appear to be key.

What do the smugglers in my study look like? Court documents and sentences are not particularly good sources with respect to analysing lifestyles the perspectives of the entrepreneurs, although they do make a reasonably valuable contribution. They reveal a little about who the criminals are. We find a cluster of persons with different backgrounds. Quite a few are unemployed, with a string of prior sentences, often for drug-related crimes. The businessman is rare in my material, but he does exist. The businessmen in my material could be described as the more shady type. They often have connections to the drug world, cooperate with known criminals and use drugs.

A rather large group can be labelled "treasure-seekers", these are the ones who want to earn a little extra by smuggling hash and are often used as couriers. This is a rather motley group of pensioners, former hotel directors, students, bingo hall owners and others. Quite a few who try their luck in trafficking seem to be in financial trouble.

The common smuggler, in my material, is a rather well known figure in criminology. Their smuggling activity is characterised by their amateurish and clumsy approach. The professional criminal and the businessman are rarely evident. There could be two reasons to account for this: one is that most of the sentences are the result of the surveillance of known criminals. In this way, the police apprehend criminals who are already well known. These may be the most central actors in the hash trafficking to Norway, although we frankly do not know this for certain. The Norwegian hash market is much smaller than the majority of the foreign ones.

Accordingly, the level of professionalism can be expected to be lower than it is in larger markets. It would be nearly impossible to maintain an ongoing large-scale trade in hash; concealing such activity over time proves very difficult. At the same time, it seems rather naive to believe that large and professional traders that, through luck and ability, keep their import hidden from police and customs don't exist, even in Norway[14].

References

Adler, P.A. 1993. *Wheeling and Dealing : An ethnography of an upper-level drug dealing and smuggling community.* 2nd ed. New York, Colombia University Press

Christie, N. & K. Bruun 1985. *Den gode fiende : Narkotikapolitikk i Norden.* Oslo, Universitetsforlaget

Desroches, F.J. 2005. *The Crime That Pays : Drug Trafficking and Organized Crime in Canada.* Toronto, Canadian Scholars' Press Inc.

Dorn, N., K. Murji & N. South 1992. *Traffickers. Drug Markets and Law Enforcement.* London, Routledge

Duyne, P.C. van 1993. "Organized crime and business crime-enterprises in the Netherlands". *Crime, Law and Social Change* 19

---

[14] There may be parallels with the smugglers of alcohol. There are rumours that the big boys that were never apprehended by the police but retired before being caught. There are similar stories in the hash market; determining what truth is and what is not is more or less impossible. Gross' book details a telling story from the US where he clearly states that more or less everyone sooner or later gets caught and adjust to this, the chapter of which is tellingly entitled "Until we get Caught" (Gross 1992).

Duyne, P.C. van 2006. "The Organisation of business crime". Duyne, P.C. van, A. Maljevic, M. van Dijck, K. von Lampe and J. Harvey eds.: *The Organisation of Crime for Profit*. Nijmegen, Wolf Legal Publishers

Duyne, P.C. van & M. Levi 2005. *Drugs and Money : Managing the drug trade and crime-money in Europe*. London, Routledge

Eck, J.E. & J.S. Gersh 2000. "Drug trafficking as a cottage industry". Natarajan & Hough eds.: *Illegal Drug Markets : From Research to Prevention Policy*. New York, Criminal Justice Press

ESPAD 2003. *Alcohol and Drug Use among Students in 35 European Countries*. Stockholm, ESPAD

Ferman, L.A, S. Henry & M. Hoyman 1987. "Preface". Ferman, Henry & Hoyman eds.: *The Informal Economy : The Annals of the American Academy of Political and Social Science* 493. London, Sage

Gaughan, J.P. & L.A. Ferman 1987. "Toward an Understanding of the Informal Economy". Ferman, Henry & Hoyman eds.: *The Informal Economy : The Annals of the American Academy of Political and Social Science* 493. London, Sage

Gross, H.K. 1992. *Drug smuggling : The forbidden book*. Boulder Colorado, Paladin Press

Johansen, P.O. 2004. *Den illegale spriten : Fra forbudstid til polstreik*. Oslo, Unipub

Johansen, P.O. 2005. "Organized Crime, Norwegian Style". Duyne, P.C. van, K. von Lampe, M. van Dijk & J.L. Newell eds.: *The Organised Crime Economy : Managing crime markets in Europe*. Nijmegen, Wolf Legal Publishers

Junninen, M. 2006. *Adventurers and Risk-Takers : Finnish Professional Criminals and their Organisations in the 1990s Cross-Border Criminality*. Helsinki, Heuni

Larsson, P. 2002. *I lovens grenseland*. Oslo, Pax

Larsson, P. 2006. "Opp i røyk! En studie av hasjimporten til Norge". Thomassen & Bjørgo eds.: *Kunnskapsutvikling i Politiet. PHS forskning 3.* Oslo, Politihøgskolen

Larsson, P. 2008a. *Organisert kriminalitet.* Oslo, Pax

Larsson, P. 2008b. "Narkotikaen er fattig mans arbeidsgiver! Organisert kriminalitet som økonomisk aktivitet". *Nordisk tidsskrift for kriminalvidenskab* 1

Paoli, L. 2002. "The paradoxes of organized crime". *Crime, Law and Social Change* 37

POD – The National Police Directorate 2005. *Project organized crime.* Oslo, POD

Sandberg, S. & W. Pedersen 2006. *Gatekapital.* Oslo, Universitetsforlaget

Schneider, F. & D.H. Enste 2003. *The Shadow Economy : An International Survey.* Cambridge, Cambridge, University Press

Skinnari, J., D. Vesterhav & L. Korsell 2007. *Vart tog alla pengarna vägen? En studie av narkotikabrottslighetens ekonomihantering.* BRÅ rapport 4

Smith-Solbakken, M. & E.M Tungland 1997. *Narkomiljøet : Økonomi, kultur og avhengighet.* Oslo, Gyldendal

Sutherland, E. 1937. *The Professional Thief : By a professional thief.* Chicago, University of Chicago Press

Vesterhav, D., J. Skinnari & L. Korsell 2007. *Narkotikadistributörer : En studie av grossisterna.* BRÅ rapport 7

Organised crime in Norway: An imported phenomenon?

Vanja Lundgren Sørli and Karsten O. F. Ingvaldsen

As Larsson (2004) has pointed out, organised crime has assumed a particularly central position in Norwegian crime policy today. A manifestation of this is that, in 2003, for the first time ever, penal provisions sanctioning organised crime appeared in the Norwegian Penal Code. Organised crime is further widely held to be very serious and considered to be one of the greatest threats of our time. This emphasis on organised crime is evident even in an NOU[1] from 2000 (NOU 2000), a public report addressing the challenges that security and emergency preparation work face regarding protection of the Norwegian society and democracy:

> Since the early 1970s, the tendency towards organised crime has steadily become more apparent (...) No Norwegian organisations similar to the Mafia organisations have been discovered, although some foreign organisations with such a structure are clearly

---
[1] Norwegian Official Reports.

operating in Norway. Several criminal groups do exist, both Norwegian and foreign, which meet the criteria of organised crime, however the structure is somewhat looser than it is in a typical Mafia.
(NOU 2000:24: art. 4.4.7, our translation)

It is uncertain what public authorities, at specific points in time, consider organised crime to be. Korsell and Hansen emphasise how the concept has various practical, economic and political functions (Korsell & Hansen 2002). Woodiwiss describes how the concept of organised crime has been historically delimited in various ways in the USA (Woodiwiss 2003). Who the enemy is and how it is characterised has changed; along with various governments and shifting political considerations. Some of these changes have concerned the kind of enemy that organised crime is conceptualised to be, for instance whether the enemy is characterised as internal or external.

According to Woodiwiss, the term organised crime was extensively used in the 1920s and 1930s in the USA (Woodiwiss 2003). The enemy was considered to be internal. Initially it also incorporated the legal aspect of society such as the police, politicians, judges, lawyers and business life. In that respect, the concept of organised crime also referred to crime that heavily featured corruption. From the 1950s onwards, the spotlight was turned upon more external enemies, to a greater degree. This stage:

(D)e-emphasised the part played by the 'respectable society' and suggested that a conspiracy of Italians

known as the Mafia dominated most organised crime in America.
(Woodiwiss 2003, 15)

This profile was further cultivated during the Reagan administration in the 1980s. The enemy now became "Forces outside mainstream American culture" (ibid, 17), thus the enemy was considered to be external.

The international regulation work as a whole against organised crime is considered by Nadelmann (1993) to be a consequence of American criminal political exportation. The Americans have been a dominant supplier of the terms determining how organised crime is to be understood as well as which regulations and methods of control are to be used to combat it (Nadelmann 1993).

The international work concerning regulation and control of organised crime has also adopted as its starting point in, and been directed towards, one threat in particular. According to Savona & De Feo, this international regulation work focuses on the trans-boundary and well structured criminality *inter alia* in the form of Columbian cartels, Chinese triads, Sicilian Mafias and Russian criminal groups (Savona & De Feo 1997). These criminal groups constitute the very definition of trans-national organised crime (Sheptycki 2000; 2003). Among international criminal authorities, they are considered to be both involved in and the reason for high volumes of drug production and trafficking, robberies, illegal weapon trade, trafficking in human beings as well as corruption and blackmail (Savona & De Feo 1997).

Based upon this, we are going to more closely investigate how organised crime is manifest in Norway today. This implies that we ask: How is organised crime conceptualised; which kind of crimes does organised crime consist of; and, who are the organised criminals? We will investigate the conceptualisation and manifestation of organised crime by legislative authorities, the courts and in the presentation of organised crime in Norwegian newspaper articles.

Norwegian Authorities' Definition of Organised Crime

In 2000, the UN agreed on a convention against organised crime, designated the Vienna Convention (Korsell & Hansen 2002). Organised crime is defined in this convention. The convention is ratified by Norway and it follows that the Norwegian political and legislative authorities are obliged to regulate and control organised crime in compliance with it (Ot.prp. No. 62, 2002–2003, paragraph 1).

The previously mentioned UN convention is drawn up within the scope of international regulation and control work and defines organised crime by eleven different criteria[2]

1) Co-operation between more than two persons.
2) Each individual has defined tasks.
3) The actions are going on for a lasting or indefinite period of time.
4) The persons are making use of some kind of discipline or supervision.
5) The persons are under suspicion of serious crimes.
6) The persons are operating internationally.
7) The persons are using violence or deterrents.

---

[2] These eleven criteria are coherent with the criteria given in the document ENFOPOL 35, established as the EU definition of organised crime, EU (1997 & 1998).

8) The persons are using commercial or business-like structures.
9) The persons are involved in money laundering.
10) The persons are exerting influence on politics, media, civil service, the legal system or finance.
11) The persons are motivated by the hunt for money/power.

(Starheimsæter 2004, our translation)

In order for a given action/actor to satisfy the definiton it must be characterised by at least six of the criteria (Starheimsæter 2004). Four of these six criteria should be numbers 1, 3, 5 and 11 (ibid). From a criminological perspective, this is an extremely broad definition that encompasses a great deal (Korsell & Hansen, 2002). This is already obvious at the starting point of the four criteria being "obligatory" for a given action to be defined as organised crime. These criteria imply that more than two persons are acting together (1), that the actions have been going on for a lasting or indefinite period of time (3), that the persons are under suspicion of serious crimes, that is, in Norway the sentencing framework will be prison for at least 3 years when an actor is sentenced for the action in question (5) and that the actors are motivated by gains or access to money or power (11).

As a starting point for discussion, it may appear as though these criteria cover many actions that are regulated in the Penal Code and not committed either by one or two persons or only once. It is therefore natural to ask whether actions and milieux that are defined as organised crime or criminals were restricted at the time the UN definition was included in the Norwegian Penal Code.

The UN convention was integrated in the Norwegian Penal Code subsequent to the suggestions made by the Bondevik administration in OT.prp. No. 62, 2002–2003. They suggested that the Penal Code should have a new penal provision which would sanction organised crime. This was duly implemented by the Act of July 4th 2003 No. 78 where the (new) provision 162c was put into immediate effect. This provision is formulated as follows:

> The Penal Code §162c
>
> *He who **enters into association with someone in** order to commit an act which may be punished with imprisonment for at least 3 years, and which is to be carried out as **part of the activity of an organised criminal group**, will be convicted to prison for 3 years unless the case is subject to a stronger penal provision. An increase of the maximum penalty in case of repeated or concurrence of felonies will not be considered.*
>
> *An organised criminal group means an **organised group of three or more persons whose main intention is to commit an act that may be penalized with imprisonment for at least 3 years**, or if a considerable part of the activity consists of committing such acts.*
>
> (The Penal Code 2006, §162c;
> our translation and bold type)

A provision about increased sentences concerning acts committed as part of the activity of such a group was simultaneously introduced in the penal code.

> The Penal Code § 60a
>
> *If an offence is committed **as part of the activity of an organised criminal group**, the maximum penalty in*

the penalty clause is doubled, not exceeding 5 year's imprisonment however.

*An organised criminal group means an **organised group of three or more persons whose main intention is to commit an act that may be penalized with imprisonment for at least 3 years**, alternatively a **considerable part of the activity** consists of committing such acts.*

(The Penal Code 2006, § 60a,
our translation and bold type)

In other words, an actor who *participates in an organised criminal group and who commits a crime that will be sanctioned with more than three years of imprisonment in a court of law* may be sent to prison for three years[3] or may have their sentence doubled, with up to five years imprisonment[4] for such participation. This occurs if one or more of the following criteria are fulfilled:

a) The actor has made an agreement (that is, entered into association) with a minimum of two other persons and jointly planned to commit an act having a sentencing framework equivalent to a sentence of at least three years imprisonment *and/or*

b) the actor, together with a minimum of two others and according to agreement, has committed acts implying a sentencing framework of at least three-years-imprisonment *and/or*

---

[3] To have either made an agreement with two or more other persons to commit a criminal act or to have committed a criminal act with two or more others.

[4] To have participated in activities with two or more other persons which include punishable offences with a sentencing framework of at least three-years-imprisonment.

c) the actor, together with a minimum of two others, has participated in activities which include crimes implying sentences of at least three-years-imprisonment.

In our opinion, it appears as though the new penal adjustment of organised crime is to a large extent directed towards co-operation on criminality. The co-operation constitutes a penalty intensifying factor and is thus defined by the concept of an organised criminal group. In the Penal Code § 60a, such a group is defined as an:

> ...organised group of three or more persons who have a **main intention** of commiting an act which may be penalized with imprisonment for at least three years, or for a **considerable part of the activity** to consist of committing such acts.
> (The Penal Code § 60, our translation and bold type).

What is meant by an "organised criminal group" is, however, further delimited by the legislator's intention in introducing the law. In the OT. prp. No. 62 (2002–2003) and in connection with the new § 162c[5], the Government states the following concerning the definition of an organised (criminal) group:

> The first condition of the definition is that an 'organised group' must exist. This implies that the group must have a certain structure and duration. Mafia-like or-

---

[5] Which will constitute the basis of the definition whether or not a group is considered criminally organised.

ganisations and other professional criminal networks with ramifications in several countries will obviously fall within the definition. Groups where the connection between the participants is not close enough for them to naturally constitute an organised group, fall outside the definition. Accordingly, the provision does not apply to all cases where several individuals are acting jointly, or where several individuals are accessory to the crime. This is the case even though it may be claimed that the participants constitute a group, providing the group is not organised, such as, for example, a group of friends who have agreed to rob a bank.

When assessing whether an 'organised group' exists, whether or not an organisational or a hierarchical structure is established will be of great importance: As is whether the group has international ramifications, whether a certain job-splitting between the members has been decided, whether the group has a connection to specific premises, whether the partakers are meeting regularly and so on. The time perspective will also be of significance. The longer a group has existed, the easier it will be to define it as an organised group according to the law. Should the opposite be the case, the time perspective will be of less importance, the more organised the group is.

It is not demanded that the group has drawn up by-laws or a programme for its activities in the way that legal organisations often do. Neither is it a demand that the group is organised in any specific way.

Organised crime's detrimental effect on society is not related to the group's means of organising itself, first and foremost, but to the very fact that the members of the group are organised.
(OT. prp. No. 62 2002–2003, 96, our translation.)

In other words, an organised criminal group is not any group co-operating on crime. This implies that the legislator has used a delimitation of what should be considered organised crime as a basis. Reading the wording of the Act and the legislative history and then comparing them give us reason to claim that the activities of an "adequately organised" criminal group can be defined as organised crime provided that two or more persons have it as their main intention to commit crime, qualifying for a sentence of three-years-imprisonment or more. When assessing whether a group is adequately organised in order to be sentenced for organised crime, the following is to be considered:

- Does the group have a particular organisational or hierarchical structure?
- Does the group have international ramifications?
- Is any specific job splitting between the members agreed on within the group?
- Can the group be connected to specific premises?
- Do the members of the group meet regularly?
- The period of time the group has been organised.
- The extent of organisation within the group.

The political definition of organised crime is imported from the UN and EU, even if the criteria given in the Norwegian Penal Code also being influenced by the Norwegian political authorities and delimitated during the legislative process. Norwegian political and legislative authorities have delimited in some areas the definition of organised crime. Despite these delimitations the Penal code is not very simplistic with respect to the definition of what organised crime consists of. The legal definition of organised crime will thus eventually be a function of how the Penal Code's § 60a is practiced by the Courts.

The Court's Delimitation of Organised Crime

To acquire an understanding of how the Penal Code § 60a is practiced by the Court and how organised crime adjudicated in Norway therefore manifests itself, we have collected sentences where this article is included in the indictments. The judicial material consists of two data sets.

The first set comprises all of the District Court sentences in which § 60a is a part of the indictment and which appeared when searching on the Lovdata[6]. The other data set consists of the criminal law-decisions (acquittals and convictions) for the year 2007 which were dealt with by Oslo District Court and where the indictments contain § 60a.[7]

---

[6] Lovdata (http://www.lovdata.no) is an authorised, public website where information about legal work and decisions, the Laws of Norway, court decisions and so on are accessible to the public. Information on court decisions is anonymous. Date of reading is 07.07.2008

[7] We have studied the sentences where the Penal Code § 60a is part of the indictments, since in Norway there has only been one sentence where the Penal code § 162c has been part of the indictments. The person was acquitted for crimes according to the Penal Code § 162c.

The Lovdata selection consists of eighteen cases from various District Courts, the bulk of which are from Oslo District Court. The sentences are from the period 2004 to 2008. In six of the cases, the prosecuting authority did not win acceptance for any of the counts containing § 60a. In twelve cases, the prosecuting authority completely or partly won acceptance in relation to § 60a. Among these, the prosecuting authority received approval concerning § 60a in eight cases for all persons prosecuted according to the article. In four of the cases the prosecuting authority did not win acceptance according to § 60a with regard to one or more persons.

Consequently, the Lovdata selection comprises twelve criminal proceedings where organised crime is adjudicated, as well as six cases where the prosecuting authority's claim of penalty aggravation according to § 60a on organised crime is altogether dismissed by the Court. The twelve cases do not constitute a precise expression of the volume of organised crime that falls within the law. Not all sentences given by the Norwegian Courts relating to certain breaches of the law are included in the Lovdata. The selection of sentences in Lovdata will also be a function of cases that the police register/investigate. Nevertheless, this selection gives us an indication of the volume. The selection of sentences from Oslo District Court provides a more accurate description.

The Oslo District Court selection is made by reviewing each and every one of the 996 litigations adjudicated in 2007 by a court consisting of one expert judge and two lay judges. In only five of these 996 litigations was the Penal Code § 60a included in the indictment. In these five cases, the prosecuting authority completely or partly won acceptance in relation to § 60a.

The data set does not include cases adjudicated by one judge. In such cases (where one expert judge adjudicates) an unreserved confession from the defendant exists and other evidence supports this. It is highly unlikely that a defendant risking up to five extra years imprisonment on the basis of § 60a, will make a full confession and want their case referred to a court consisting of one expert judge. Consequently, there is reason to believe that the five convictions in the selection concerning § 60a indeed are representative of the amount of cases adjudicated according to § 60a by Oslo District Court in 2007.

These five litigations constitute approximately 0.5% of the 996 cases dealt with by Oslo District Court in 2007. As we shall see later on, in most of the cases in the Lovdata selection, organised crime which is adjudicated relates to the Penal Code § 162 regarding processing, import/export, trafficking and storing of narcotics. This also applies to the selection from the Oslo district court where three out of five cases are connected to narcotics.

Of the 996 cases in the selection from a court consisting of one expert judge and two lay judges, 407, or more than 40%, contained one or more counts according to § 162. Among the cases dominated by drug felonies, that most sentences pertaining to § 60a are related to, the court thus judges 3 out of 407 drug cases to be organised crime. This implies that organised crime is linked to 0.7% of the drug cases adjudicated by Oslo District Court in the year 2007. In other words, organised crime, as the court defines it, constitutes a very small part of these criminal offences.

What then does the adjudicated organised crime consist of? Among the twelve cases in the Lovdata selection, organised crime is linked to drug felonies in eight. The other four cases involve "skimming" (reading equipment is installed on cash dispensers and account-holders' accounts are subsequently abused); fraudulent use of false credit cards; aggravated robbery; as well as one incident of human trafficking combined with forced prostitution. As mentioned earlier, in three of five cases in the District Court selection, drug crimes also come into focus. Consequently, adjudicated organised crime is fairly narrow since most of the adjudicated cases are linked to the same category of crimes: drug felonies.

The sentences can also tell us what connection the convicted persons had to the organised criminal group responsible for the planning, organisation and implementation of the crimes. In total, 51 persons, amongst them 1 woman, were convicted according to § 60a of the Penal Code. The court characterises 26 of these as the principals because they had a fixed and lasting position within the organised criminal group. They represented the driving force of the group. 25 of the convicted persons were considered to be more peripheral in their relation to the group. They did not have a fixed position in the group; their illegal co-operation with the group was more *ad hoc*. They co-operated with the group on merely one or a few isolated illegal operations.

Another interesting question pertains to which criminal groups are involved in these cases. Were they Norwegian or foreign criminal groups? In only 2 out of 12 cases, we can talk of a Norwegian group, meaning persons living and residing permanently in Norway. In by far the majority of cases, that is the remaining 10, the court establishes that the criminal group is either completely or primarily located abroad.

How is § 60a in the Penal Code put into practice by the Norwegian judicial authorities? As so few cases are judged to be organised crime in accordance with § 60a in the Penal Code, this is also related to the fact that the court is practicing the law strictly.

It requires a fair amount of justification in order for the court to describe a group of people who have committed felonies as an organised criminal group. This appears *inter alia* in some of the six cases in the Lovdata selection where the prosecuting authority won no acceptance in terms of the indictments according to § 60a. In one of the cases, four men were convicted for importing 40 kilograms of amphetamine into Norway. They consisted of a group that had co-operated on the import, it was well planned, the four had separate and distinct roles and the group was internationally rooted. However, the group was connected only to this one specific breach of the law. The court did not therefore find that:

> (T)he group which the four defendants in that respect constitute has the adequate structure, organisation and duration for § 60a in the Penal Code to be applicable.
> (Our translation).

On the other hand, it requires far less to be convicted for having assisted a criminal group that one is not part of. This explains why as many as 25 persons were convicted according to § 60a, based on tasks they had carried out in connection with criminal groups they were judged to not be members of. The reason is that the court is practicing a dimension of due care. The 25 persons were convicted according to § 60a because the court found it to be established as probable that they knew, or ought to have known, that they participated in criminality that was part of a criminal group's practice. Whether a person is a part of a criminal group or is co-operating with one in their capacity as an outsider, is therefore of no consequence in terms of being convicted according to § 60a or otherwise.

The relationship to such a criminal group, however, is important with respect to how stringently the court applies the element of increased penalty included in the Act. The greater the degree of involvement a person with such a criminal group has, the longer their potential additional custodial sentence.

Imported organised crime

As mentioned earlier, a fundamental feature related to the organised crime adjudicated is the fact that it originates from foreign countries. Mainly, it is organised criminal groups located abroad which are involved in these cases; more specifically, most of these groups are located in the Netherlands.

The same foreign aspect is also expressed by the fact that the majority of the 51 individuals convicted according to § 60a in the Penal Code are apparently foreigners without Norwegian citizenships and with domiciles abroad. Even if the public duplicates of the sentences in the Lovdata selection are made anonymous by removing personal data in the indictments, the descriptions in various parts of the majority of the convictions clearly indicate the citizenships and domiciles of the accused [8].

Furthermore, it seems as though the share of foreigners is greatest amongst the persons described by the court as the principals:

---

[8] In the convictions, there are descriptions of the criminal acts, actors involved, places where the actions have taken place, the actors› domicile and even a few names of actors other than the convicted. An analysis based on this makes it possible to draw conclusions about the nationality of those convicted and whether they had non-Norwegian roots.

permanent members and therefore of significance to the organised criminal groups. The Norwegian actors involved in the acts of organised crime are described by the court as being outside of the organised criminal groups.

Norwegian organised crime, in the sense of organised criminal groups located in Norway, whose primary members are Norwegians with their domicile in Norway, is conspicuous by its absence. This is scarcely due to any selective form of control. There is little reason to believe that organised criminal groups located on Norwegian grounds will escape the long arm of the law to any greater extent than groups based outside of Norway. Indeed, it is probably that the case is quite the reverse. It is a well known criminological finding that, the farther away the crime, the less likely it is that the police will solve it. The police have more ready access to information about local offenders in addition to basic previous knowledge about them.

This picture of organised crime therefore falls within the scope of what Woodiwiss characterises as the external enemy (Woodiwiss 2003). It is criminality that has its origin outside the country's boundaries, in other words that it is imported from abroad, which constitutes the organised crime adjudicated in Norway. However, we do not entirely follow the author's line of reasoning. His perspective seems too pure and definite as he seems to be of the opinion that the authorities' understanding and delimitation of organised crime at any time is almost exclusively a function of which political oppurtunities the consept is perceived to offer. In our opinion the understanding of the authorities and the court especially, of organised crime must be considered a reflection of other conditions as well.

The picture that comes to light from the adjudicated sentences is, at any rate, a result of two conditions. The legislation in question is imported from the UN and the EU. The main objective of this legislation is the apprehention of criminality with international ramifications. The definition of organised crime encompasses the international aspect as an essential factor and it is therefore not surprising that the adjudicated organised crime is of an international nature.

However, Norwegian criminal organised groups will not be precluded on grounds related to definitions. Nevertheless, the fact that they are undetectable may presumably result from organised crime run from Norway frequently being of such a nature that it falls outside the court's delimitation of what organised crime is. This is so due to two conditions. In part, it lacks international ramifications and, in a number of cases, has neither the relatively strict structure, nor the duration demanded by the court. The dominant type of organised crime in Norway has for quite a long time consisted of activities in the Norwegian illegal alcohol market (Johansen 1996, 2008): various forms of alcohol smuggling and illicit distillation. The smuggling of spirits can be said to have some international ramifications because the Norwegian smugglers are dependant upon a certain degree of co-operation with foreign actors in order to gain access to spirits and be able to bring the spirits into the country as safely as possibly. However, the Norwegian smuggling of spirits has, over the course of the last few years, been relatively subdued owing to dramatic deaths in relation to incidents involving methanol-containing spirits, (Johansen 2004; Lundgren Sørli 2005). Based on this, some of the actors involved in smuggling have since switched to the smuggling of wine and beer.

Norwegian illicit distilling is to be viewed as an entirely Norwegian form of criminality (Johansen 1994; 2004). The illegal spirit is both produced, and mainly sold in, Norway. This is crime without international ramifications and part of what has been regarded as Norwegian organised crime, (Johansen 1994). Other types of organised crime also exist in Norway: the Norwegian police have defined a robbery-milieu, consisting of up to 20 individuals robbing banks, post offices and secure vehicles transporting money. To a rather large extent, this milieu is of Norwegian origin (Larsson 2008).

There are, however, some milieux in Norway, which are connected to organised crime and have international roots to some degree. Some of these milieux are connected to the smuggling and sale of drugs. The A and B gangs are among the more important narcotics smugglers in Norway (Ingvaldsen & Larsson 2007). The police have identified 53 members of these gangs in total. The groups have good contacts in both the Netherlands and Denmark – used for the import and dealing of cannabis. Certain biker groups are also considered important in the import and dealing of cannabis in Norway (Ingvaldsen & Larsson 2007). These groups have only few members although some of them have convictions for smuggling cannabis or amphetamines.

There are also a few examples of foreign organised criminal groups operating in Norway. One such example is Lithuanian groups whose main activity thus far has been organised shoplifting (Larsson 2008). These more or less internationally rooted groups only number a few and the amount of members is limited. It therefore remains accurate to say that, when seen from a criminological perspective, organised crime in Norway has international connections or roots only to a limited extent (Larsson 2008).

Moreover, Johansen characterises Norwegian organised crime in the main to be quite unlike the criminality committed within well-structured organisations (Johansen 1996, 2008). In his study, Larsson (2008) describes organised crime in Norway in a similar manner. One example is the aforementioned A and B gangs. These gangs are not well-structured organisations; instead they can be characterized as networks comprising friends in their teens that have graduated to organised crime, over time. The point is that the criminality is committed within relations so flexible and loosely founded that the strict organisation model which is the foundation of sentences for committing organised crime in Norway proves unsuitable for the bulk of Norwegian organised crime. Crimes committed in connection with relatively loose and passing networks would therefore be a more appropriate criminological description[9] of present organised crime in Norway (Johansen 2008, Larsson 2008).

A substantial part of Norwegian organised crime, as understood criminologically, consequently lacks the international ramifications, the strict organisation along with stability and permanency related to the group, which the court demands in order to consider it organised crime. In that respect, the images of organised crime which the court provides are not particularly fitting when describing the picture of organised crime in Norway.

Accordingly it proves interesting to ask how organised crime appear in the media: most people's main source of knowledge about criminality.

---

[9] Korsell & Hansen (2002) describe organised crime in Sweden in a similar manner.

Media presentations of organised crime

How is organised crime presented in Norwegian newspapers? We searched A-text[10] for articles on organised crime published in the Norwegian newspapers *Aftenposten* and *Dagbladet*[11] over the course of one year[12]. We searched for articles containing the phrase "organised crime" and defined published stories where the the medium, the victim, the victim's lawyer or representative, the police, the prosecuting authorities or political authorities were mentioning organised crime, as of interest. In total, "organised crime" was found in 137 articles in *Aftenposten* and 55 articles in *Dagbladet*. From these, we made a selection focusing on stories[13] in which where the previously mentioned actors employed the term "organised crime" to describe or categorise particular actions. Our final selection consisted of 52 articles published in *Aftenposten* and 19 published in *Dagbladet*.

In terms of addressing the questions concerning which activities are characterised as organised crime, which actions appear to be serious because they are linked to organised crime or are serious because they are being organised, then the answers vary according

---

[10] A-text is a media-archive of all published Norwegian newspaper-articles. This is electronic and available to paying subscribers. http: www.retriever.no

[11] Two of the greatest newspapers in Norway are both in tabloid format and are released daily, with a minimum of one edition per day. *Aftenposten* was earlier categorised as a conservative newspaper and *Dagbladet* as a liberal newspaper.

[12] Published in *Aftenposten* and *Dagbladet* between July 7th 2007 and July 7th 2008.

[13] In this context, published stories comprise newsarticles, magazine articles, editorials, comments, debate articles and NTB (the Norwegian news agency) information.

to the newspaper in which the articles are published. In *Dagbladet*, violations of the law of securities trading, trafficking in human beings, insider trading, money laundering, debt-collector activity, receiving, credit card fraud, weapon trade, smuggling and dealing of narcotics and aggravated robberies carried out of "gangs" are characterised as organised crime. *Dagbladet* also draws attention to money laundering at fertility clinics; this is presented as a kind of activity which organised criminal groups are behind. The newspaper also draws attention to connections between the security industry and organised criminal groups.

In *Aftenposten*, the term "organised crime" is used to describe the same activities, with the exception of money laundering at fertility clinics. In addition, theft of works of art and cultural relics, criminality committed by Bikers[14], computer crime, data criminality, network fraud, production of cocaine and cannabis as well as gang confrontations are characterised as organised crime. A connection is made between organised crime and actors taking nude photographs of children in Norway and Eastern Europe; between violation of the law pertaining to social security, the law pertaining to VAT, the Food Law, the Accounting Act, the Tax Law and organised crime[15]; between theft of vehicle registration number plates and also car fraud and organised crime; between residential burglary and organised crime; as well as pirate taxi activities and organised crime. Furthermore, animal protection extremists are described as "organised criminal activists", tagging as actions carried out by "organised crews", and the taxi trade as an arena of extensive organised crime.

---

[14] Members of particular clubs of (motor-)bikers.
[15] The actual organised crime in this particular article is also referred to as a "kebab Mafia".

When asking how organised crime is presented the material reveals that organised crime is a theme in roughly five categories of articles:

I: Published articles in which media or other actors characterise various actions as organised crime.

"Organised crime" here is generally presented via a certain action or process of action and will commonly be a report on a current case, an apprehension, an indictment, a remand or a court case.

Dagbladet featured nine stories[16] that either completely or partly have this theme; *Aftenposten* features eighteen such stories[17]. *Aftenposten* exemplifies it when, in conjunction with a main presentation in the Economy section, beneath the heading "Granted guarantees and loans" (Frafjord 2008) there is a fact box about "The Inside Case in Acta" which informs the reader that seven persons are charged in the greatest inside case ever in Norway and that the "mafia provision" (the Penal Code § 60a) has been applied for the first time in an insider case[18]. Something that will duly increase (the upper) sentencing framework (should the Defendant be sentenced) from six to eleven years-imprisonment. Furthermore, the alleged principal and their closest family, who stand accused in the same case, are presented. The principal is presented by name and the relations of other persons to the principal are established. In this

---

[16] Some stories are thematised in such a way that they must be placed in two categories analytically. That is why the amount of published articles does not correspond with the final amount in the selection. This applies to both newspapers.
[17] See note above.
[18] We would like to point out that for the time being the case has not been adjudicated, although the prosecuting authorities have elected to charge seven persons (in addition) according to the Penal Code § 60a.

specific case, the "organised criminals" are Norwegian. This is in contrast to the majority of articles of this kind in both newspapers; in which, organised crime is principally carried out by actors of nationalities other than Norwegian.

II: Published articles where media or other actors use the term "organised" to denote that a category of actions are perceived as serious.

In these articles, a specific kind of criminality or a specific person's or group's crimes are characterised as "organised" and it is evident from the text that the violation also is understood to be serious by media or the interviewee describing the action.

Dagbladet has six articles that are wholly or in part classified in such a manner. In one example, the headline is "Grossly Exploited by Human-Traffickers" (Kristiansen Kvaale, Klungtveit & Slaaen 2008). *Dagbladet* refers to the police taking action against 20 different places in Oslo during the days previous to the publishing of the story, arresting 58 women whose identities and residence permits will be checked while 18 persons are to face far more serious charges. According to the "investigators[19]", these persons have organised the transport of the prostitutes into Norway as well as arranged apartments for them. The article highlights the fact that investigators from different countries are involved in the criminal investigation, that the women according to the opinion of the police are deprived of the main part of their income by a central network. This central network has been organising the trafficking of prostitutes to Norway, some as young as 16 years old. It is pointed out in the article that this is

---

[19] Referred to with anonymous references.

an organised, albeit complex network with ramifications which affect "many different countries".

Aftenposten had nineteen published stories that can be themed in such a manner. One of these was presented in Aftenposten on 5th April 2008, with the headline "The accountant received eight years for tax fraud", (Haakaas & Sæter 2008). The article was based on the fact that the Supreme Court summarily dismissed the appeal of an accountant who was convicted to eight years of imprisonment. The first judge to pass a sentence was quoted as having stated that the appealing party, convicted of criminal conduct was characterised by "systematic, organised, extensive and prolonged activities with the purpose of rendering professional assistance to the taxi owners aiming at tax evasion". Based upon a separate reading of the Interlocutory Appeals Committee's decision, it is clear that the adjective "organised" is used in a descriptive manner and emphasises the seriousness of the felony from the Supreme Court's perspective. This is regularly emphasised in the other newspaper articles in this category[20].

The serious "organised" crimes carried out by foreign actors can be found in numerous articles. Nevertheless, more Norwegians than foreign actors are involved in the actual crimes in cases where

---

[20] Vanja Lundgren Sørli has an ongoing project dealing with economical crimes in the Norwegian taxi trade (Lundgren Sørli 2008). The term "organised", used as a description of financial crimes committed within the taxi business is recurring in the interviews with Økokrim (The Norwegian National Authority for the Investigation and Prosecution of Economic and Environmental Crime), the tax office's supervision team and (previously) The National Insurance Service's section of abuse. The interviewees' opinions on whether financial crimes should be perceived as "organised" criminality or "organised crime" vary, but when it comes to an interpretation there is little doubt that crimes are regarded as serious when described as organised.

nationality is not mentioned. It can thus be inferred that the actor is a Norwegian. In other words, the serious and "organised" criminality is not carried out by foreigners/external enemies, to the same extent as the violations of the law characterised as "organised crime" are.

III: Published articles in which organised crime is being characterised as a threat by media or other actors.

The threatening picture emerges by attention being drawn to increasing levels of organised crime, the fact that organised crime belongs to an extremely serious category of crimes or to the consequences and social damage that organised crime implies. Actors warning of the threat constitute the media, the police, organisations or politicians. Organised crime partly appears in such contexts as an argument for increasing grants to a particular group, investigation method or body. In part, the threat of organised crime is also used as an argument for altered (and especially tightened) legislation and sentencing frameworks, capacity for more prisoners, altered control routines[21] or intensified investigations, supervision and greater focus on the discussion of various types of criminality or groups.

Dagbladet has three articles that can partly or completely be classified as this, *Aftenposten* has eighteen. One of the last-mentioned is taken from *Aftenposten* on 2nd October 2007, in which Økokrim[22] beneath the headline "Fooling with flirt and fantasies – Nigerian swindlers become more and more devious"

---

[21] Such as telephone surveillance linked to the directive on data saving, or quite other special arenas of supervision, for example supervision of driving schools for emergency vehicles.

[22] The Norwegian National Authority for the Investigation and Prosecution of Economic and Environmental Crimes.

points out that Norwegians are steadily being swindled out of more money. It goes on to say that, in 2007, Norwegians were tricked out of far more than the 100 million kroner[23] that was lost in 2006; at the same time, the article warns against contact with Nigerian swindlers. "They are not mere swindlers, they are involved in trafficking in human beings, weapon trade, drug trafficking and in most types of organised crime" states *Aftenposten* (Midthun 2007).

The threat constituted by organised crime in the articles is determined to come mainly from abroad. Articles of this kind in both the daily newspapers communicate a sense of threatening organised crime (not yet established in Norway) having its origin in foreign countries or cultures other than the most common Norwegian one. The stories give the impression that "we" have to brace ourselves against "them" – that is, the danger of Norway being invaded by organised criminals.

IV: Published articles where either the defence or the alleged perpetrator criticise the police or media for establishing connections between the actions of an actor/actors and organised crime.

Dagbladet has published a case that can be classified thus; while *Aftenposten* ran two such articles. The article in *Dagbladet* is an illustrative example. Beneath the headline, "Proper press practice?" (Reiss-Andersen 2008), *Dagbladet* is criticised for defending The Press Association's Expert Committee[24] (PFU) following a woman being associated with organised crime. The woman was indicted for

---

[23] Approximately 11.5 million Euro.
[24] Pressens faglige utvalg (PFU).

receiving as a part of an organised criminal group and acquitted by the court finally. In the PFU, *Dagbladet* argued in favour of the view that practicing the principles of public access to courts of justice so that the accused was associated with a drug group and organised crime, represented a guarantee of legal security under the law for the woman. In the actual article in *Dagbladet* the arguments of *Dagbladet* are focused on and criticised.

In these articles, the actors associated with organised crime are Norwegian, while the crimes are committed by actors with foreign origin. In the three articles themselves, the indicted/acting person was acquitted or claimed to be innocent.

V: Published articles that level criticism at lack of investigation a.s.o. in actual cases.

These articles argue that a lack of investigation or media coverage has the implication of a major risk of organised crime. *Dagbladet* has published two cases which wholly or partly can be categorised thus; *Aftenposten* has one such article (Stanghelle 2007). The *Aftenposten* article illustrates the point well, beneath the headline "A dangerous threat", the political editor criticises the fact that a shooting incident at the home of a journalist a year earlier remains unsolved. The editor points out that if the shooting incident is a consequence of the journalist practicing her occupation *"(...) well, then this is a matter of something far greater than a horrible experience for a skillful colleague in Dagsavisen"*. Moreover, he argues that the *"brave media are a premise for organised crime not gaining a stronger foothold in our own country"*.

The organised crime referred to in these articles is committed against Norwegian victims by unknown perpetrators. In other words, the victims are familiar and the offenders, or the enemies, are foreign or at least unknown. This in itself contributes to the concept of the organised criminal as a stranger, a foreigner or an external enemy and their actions (the organised crime) as a threat imported to Norwegian society.

Problems imported by external enemies

When asking who the organised criminals referred to in the media are, it is difficult to give an answer which is not ambiguous. The articles do not have equal structure and some articles describe several cases. The course of events, the number of apprehensions or indictments and the actors' roles in the network are all entwined. Consequently, methodical problems arise when giving an account of which actors appear, their role and which of these are presented as "organised criminals" in *Dagbladet* and *Aftenposten*.

From an analytical point of view, we can nevertheless claim that the organised crime described in the daily newspapers examined here and committed on Norwegian soil, is a category of actions that are predominantly carried out by actors of foreign or non-Norwegian cultural background. In other words, in the media we address here depict organised crime as an imported phenomenon, carried out by what Woodiwiss characterises as external enemies (Woodiwiss 2003). This implies that the media conceptualisation of organised crime both agrees with and differs from the organised crime that is then sentenced and, broadly speaking, rather badly with the Norwegian criminological literature on the subject.

Based on articles covering apprehensions and indictments, there is a relatively large proportion of women among the apprehended and the indicted.[25] This directly contradicts the court material, as well the picture painted by Per Ole Johansen derived from studies of organised crime:

> Women do take part, albeit it is in different ways in various countries and periods, but as a whole organised crime is 'the men's world', both statistically and with regard to who the dominating partner is.
> (Johansen 1996:13, our translation)

Furthermore, it is obvious that Lithuanians, Nigerians and people from Pakistan are nationalities which frequently recur in articles which comment on the nationality of the "organised criminals". In other words, in the newspapers, organised crime is apparently a problem mainly coming from abroad. This corresponds to the Lovdata selection and findings from Oslo District Court. The nationalities of the external enemies portrayed in media, is not, however, in accordance with those highlighted in the court material alluding to organised criminal groups' origin and localization.

When viewed from a criminological perspective, organised crime has seldom been associated with specific foreign ethnic or national groups in Norway. Some exceptions undoubtedly exist: Ingvaldsen and Larsson exemplify this with their discussion of drug-trafficking in Norway (Ingvaldsen and Larsson 2007), Snertingdal with her description of the heroin trade (Snertingdal 2007), and Larsson with his account of Lithuanian groups who

---

[25] According to the media, the reason for this is that many women have indeed been apprehended and at times indicted for the trafficking of people.

commit organised thefts (Larsson 2008), although this refers to specific empirical contexts.

As mentioned earlier, Norwegian organised crime has traditionally involved the smuggling and illlegal distillation of alcohol, and there have been no *major* changes in the variations of organised criminal actions in Norway since the 1990s (Johansen 2008). These crimes are typically committed by Norwegians (Johansen 1985, 1994, 2004), and are not mentioned in the newspaper-articles. More recent forms of Norwegian organised crimes, such as biker groups and the robbery milieu (Larsson 2008) are mentioned, but do not merit much attention.

Analytically, the media's presentation of organised crime and "organised" criminality is vast. Organised crime constitutes a wide category of actions and one may well get the impression that, relatively, we have a great deal of organised crime on Norwegian soil. When taken to its extremes, the category of actions dubbed organised crime in the media goes from "tagging" to people trafficking. This is neither consistent with the court material, nor with the already mentioned criminological understanding of Norwegian organised crime. Organised crime is, from a criminological perspective, traditionally understood as smuggling and the distillation of alcohol (Johansen 1996), it has also recently been associated with specific areas of the drug market, (Johansen 1996; Ingvaldsen & Larsson 2007) and the robbery milieu (Ingvaldsen & Larsson 2007, Larsson 2008). It follows that the threatening picture that appears in the media is considerably broader than the threats organised crime seems to constitute according to our court material and criminological analysis. This is so despite the fact that the legislation preceding the court material is a product of a threatening evaluation emphasising that "from the early 1970s the tendency towards organised crime has been continuously more obvious" (NOU 2004:24, paragraph 4.4.7).

In this context, we will not comment on the reasons for the presentation, to Norwegian society, of the increasing threat of a non-registered, non-adjudicated organised crime that is depicted as an external enemy and an imported phenomenon by the media, politicians, various organisations and the emphasis of the police. Instead, here, we will simply underline the fact that the daily newspapers, amongst other agents, make organised crime appear such when it is presented in the media.

Concluding remarks

In this article, we have described and analysed how organised crime is presented in legislation, the application of law and Norwegian newspapers. Our main objective has been to elucidate whether organised crime in Norway – subsequent to the penal provisions instituted in the year 2003 – should be characterised as an international phenomenon, or (even more extremely) viewed as an external enemy by these actors. The answer to this question is yes, when looking into the intention of Norwegian legislation, the application of law and the media presentations of organised crime.

Based exclusively on the text of the statute, organised crime is not necessarily an international phenomenon. Nevertheless, it is clear that when considering the legislator's intention of the text of the Law, one has to take the Norwegian Penal Code § 162c and § 60a into account – these define how organised crime should be understood judicially. These are provisions with clear international sources in the UN and EU. According to Nadelmann, the legislation work aiming at regulating organised crime within the systems of the UN and the EU may be further understood in terms of American exportation of judicial priorities and solutions (Nadelmann 1993).

Accordingly, it is only natural that the picture of registered crime in Norway in the form of Norwegian court material presents organised crime as trans-boundary and well structured. The court material depicts organised crime in Norway as something that features organisations primarily of foreign origin. In the media, the organisation aspect is not emphasised in the same manner or to the same extent, however organised crime is mainly classed as crimes committed by actors involving groups of persons, networks or organisations either from abroad or with foreign origin.

Such a picture, from a criminological position, however, is hardly accurate as an overarching description of organised crime in Norway. The juridical descriptions, as well as the presentations by the media, leave out what has been perceived as specifically Norwegian types of organised crime. Norwegian organised crime is internationally rooted in only a limited sense and it does not fit well with the rigid organisation model which the Penal Code § 60a is based upon. As such, the presentation of Norwegian organised crime by the courts and the newspapers is rather selective.

In that respect, organised crime in Norway is not mainly an imported phenomenon: in the sense that such types of crimes are committed primarily by foreigners and people of non-Norwegian ethnic origin. First and foremost, it is the legislation regarding organised crime that has been imported: internationally rooted legislation based upon threat evaluations and an understanding of criminality which are relevant to Norway only in a limited sense.

References

EU 1997. Council of the European Union, 6204/2/97. ENFOPOL 35, Brussels 21 April 1997

Ingvaldsen, K. & P. Larsson 2007. "Hvitvasking på det norske verdipapirmarkedet : Om hvitvaskingens betingelser".

Magnusson, D. & H. Sjögren eds.: *Skatteundandragande, penningtvätt och organiserad brottslighet.* Forskningsrapport 19. Stockholm, Handelshögskolan i Stockholm

Johansen, P.O. 1985. *Brennevinskrigen : En krønike om forbudstidens Norge.* Oslo, Gyldendal

Johansen, P.O. 1994. *Markedet som ikke ville dø : Forbudstiden og de illegale alkoholmarkedene i Norge og USA.* Oslo, Rusmiddeldirektoratet

Johansen, P.O. 1996. *Nettverk i gråsonen : Et perspektiv på organisert kriminalitet.* Oslo, Ad Notam

Johansen, P.O. 2004. *Den illegale spriten : Fra forbudstid til polstreik.* Oslo, Unipub

Johansen, P.O. 2008. "Organisert kriminalitet – Hva nå?". *Nordisk Tidsskrift for kriminalvidenskap* 3

Korsell, L.E. & H.Ö. Hansen 2002. *Organiserad brottslighet – lösa maskor eller fasta nätverk.* BRÅ rapport 7

Larsson, P. 2004. "Organisert kriminalitet – myter og realiteter. Om behovet for en kunnskapsorientert analytisk tilnærming til den organiserte kriminaliteten". *PHS Forskning 2.* Oslo, Politihøgskolen

Larsson, P. 2008. *Organisert kriminalitet.* Oslo, Pax

Lundgren Sørli, V. 2005. *In a Man's World : Tolkninger av lovbrudd gjort i langtransportens yrkeskontekst.* Avhandlingsserie 16. Stockholm, Kriminologiska Institutionen

Lundgren Sørli, V. 2008. "Svartkjøring i norsk drosjenæring: Kulturelle forståelser". *Disorder in Urban Public Space : Resistance or Crime? Economic Crime, Organised Crime and Corruption"* Forssa, Rapport fra NSfK's 50. forskerseminar

Nadelmann, E. 1993. *Cops Across Borders : The Internationalization of U.S. Criminal Law Enforcement.* University Park, PN: Pennsylvania State University Press

NOU 2000:24. *Et sårbart samfunn : Utfordringer for sikkerhets- og beredskapsarbeidet i samfunnet.* Oslo, Justis- og politidepartementet, Norges Offentlige Utredninger

Ot. prp. Nr. 62, 2002-2003. *Om lov om endringer i straffeloven og straffeprosessloven mv.* Oslo, Lovdata

Savona, E.U & M.A. De Feo 1997. "International Money Laundering Trends and Prevention/Control Policies". Savona ed.: *Responding to Money Laundering : International Perspectives.* Harwood Academic Publishers

Sheptycki, J. 2000. "Policing the virtual launderette : Money laundering and global governance". Sheptycki, J. ed.: *Issues in transnational policing.* London, Routledge

Sheptycki, J. 2003. "Global Law enforcement as a protection Racket : Some sceptical notes on transnational organised crime as an object of global governance". Edwards, A. & P. Gill eds.: *Transnational Organised Crime : Perspectives on Global Security.* London and New York, Routledge

Snertingdal, M.I. 2007. *Kalkulerende kjeltringer eller offer for omstendighetene? En kvalitativ studie av heroinomsettingens utvikling og aktører.* SIRUS rapport 1. Oslo, Statens institutt for rusmiddelforskning

Starheimsæter, J. 2004. "Organisert miljøkriminalitet i EU". *Miljøkrim* 1

The Penal Code 2006 [Straffeloven 2006]. *Alminnelig borgerlig Straffelov : Lov av 22. mai nr. 10, 1902.* Trondheim, Lovdata

Woodiwiss, M. 2003. "Transnational organised crime : The global reach of an American concept". Edwards, A. & P. Gill eds.: *Transnational Organised Crime Perspectives on Global Security*. London and New York, Routledge

Newspapers

Frafjord, E. 2008. "Delte ut garantier og lån". *Aftenposten* 26/6/08

Haakaas, E. & S. Kjetil 2008. "Regnskapsføreren fikk åtte år for skattesvik". *Aftenposten* 5/4/08

Kristiansen Kvaale, Klungtveit & Slaaen 2008. "Grovt utnyttet av menneskesmuglere". *Dagbladet* 19/6/08

Midthun, A. 2007. "Lurer med flørt og fantasier – Nigeria-svindlerne stadig mer utspekulerte". *Aftenposten* 2/10/07

Reiss-Andersen, B. 2008. "God presseskikk?". *Dagbladet* 1/6/08

Stanghelle, H. 2007. "En farlig trussel". *Aftenposten* 12/7/07

Internet

EU 1998. [Date of reading 15/6/2008]. Council Resolution on the Prevention of Organised Crime (OJ C 408 of 29/12/1998). http: www.unicri.it/wwd/justice/docs/TransnationalCrime/1998_408_ Council_Resolution_20_on_organised_Crime.pdf

Lovdata 2008 [Date of reading 7/7/2008]. http://www.lovdata.no

A-tekst 2008. [Date of reading 7/7/2008]. http: //www.retriever.no

Searching the organised crime knowledge grail: Disorganised EU threat methodology

Petrus C. van Duyne

"Organised crime", excitement and knowledge

"Organised crime" is a remarkable phenomenon: it has managed to remain high on the political agenda for two decades, while the priority ranking of other topics shows a more pendulum pattern. Yet what is so interesting about "organised crime"? It is an elusive concept, a political and juridical construction and scientifically impossible to define, despite lofty and futile attempts (Van Duyne et al. 2003; Kinzig and Luczak 2004; Van Duyne & Van Dijck 2007; Von Lampe 2001). It would be worthwhile to make a general review of the "phenomenon" over the past half a century in order to address one basic question: (except for the rhetoric) "What is new?" Not very much really: crime-entrepreneurs still smuggle and extort, they are occasionally thwarted by the police or killed by their fellow criminals. Granted, some contraband commodities and illegal opportunities have changed. Given the simple economic fact that like any trade, crime-trade is based on price differences, mainly between countries, the purported phenomena is cross-border, and that has been the case since time immemorial. When one studies the many case descriptions that are commonly subsumed under this heading – all forms of trafficking (mainly drugs, although other commodities also) or the "protection industry" (illegal power structures) – one is struck by their banality. Organised criminals are human too (Van Duyne 2000). For good reason, I teach my students that the history of organised crime is a history of banalities, of the perpetrators as well as the police. Nevertheless, "organised crime" is experienced as an entertaining thrill, which may have contributed to the political miracle of it still not passing its expiration date, more than its supposed threat.

For policy makers and law enforcement agencies this state of affairs feels uneasily: it is difficult to reconcile entertaining excitement with the proclaimed seriousness of the phenomenon. But these uneasy feelings are ambiguous: excitement attracts public and political attention or keeps it at a desired level of political importance. However, "organised crime" as elaborated in policy papers and international literature[1], is definitely no laughing matter: it is a serious matter, a threat. However, threat images devoid of personal concrete experience tend to blur over time; how many people experience actual "organised crime" threats? For this reason, threat images have to be refreshed and assessed regularly. Another stated reason for producing threat assessments is for strategic decision-making; however, it is hard to find an unambiguous publicised example of a report leading explicitly to a strategic law-enforcement decision. Despite this lack of evidence, threat assessments are also a serious matter for which one needs knowledge

---

[1] For a European overview, see Fijnaut and Paoli (2004), in which 35 authors present their view on "organised crime" and the relevant counter-policy.

about the phenomenon. Therefore, today, the phrase: *knowledge based policy-making* is presented as a serious matter. That is not about flashes of insight, but a knowledge development requiring an *organisation*. In addition, for knowledge to be qualified as such, there are certain standards. The more serious social phenomena or threats are, the stricter the knowledge standards must be maintained. This applies particularly to the basic standard of transparency and accountability. Knowledge without accountability should not be qualified as such.

In this article, I shall take all these proclaimed serious matters as points of reference and investigate aspects of this organisation of knowledge about "organised crime". I shall focus on the EU and, in particular, the assessment of organised crime threats. We will find out whether these EU threat assessment activities are commensurate to the proclaimed seriousness and to knowledge standards.

Organising knowledge: a human undertaking

In an ideal world, acquiring knowledge and insight is supposed to be a serene undertaking. Such an ideal world does not exist; neither at universities, nor in the field of action where knowledge should be applied. Knowledge-building requires a great deal of social organisation, which rarely follows an orderly path. As can be observed in most inter-human undertakings, it is sloppy and disorderly. The organisation of knowledge about organised crime is no exception to this.

My first experience with knowledge-building in this field was at a meeting at Interpol in Lyons, 1991. The previous year I had published the first Dutch book on organised crime, entitled *Crime-entrepreneurs* (Van Duyne et al. 1990), which may well have contributed to my invitation to a meeting with police officers and policy-makers, all "experts".[2] Owing to a programme reshuffle, my presentation was moved to the start of the meeting. Although I did not have a definition of organised crime (nor do I have one now), I quickly compiled a couple of distinctive features, which I illustrated with examples from my research. These examples concerned the anything but bright execution of a few whole-sale smuggling operations by the highest-ranking Dutch crime-organisation at that time. I cited an example of a crew floating on the shallows and between the islands by the Dutch coast, equipped with a tourist cycling map and apparently unfamiliar with the tide phenomena. They were subsequently surprised by the low tide and became stuck in the sand. The chairman, representing the UN, amassed the suggested distinguishing features together as a form of definition for the remainder of the conference. Nevertheless, during a break he then reprimanded me for my presentation of top criminals as a bunch of incompetent perpetrators: "I must make people aware of the seriousness of this serious phenomenon, and so you cannot say this!" This awareness raising he did by raking in every token suggested as "serious organised crime": from drug trafficking in the industrialised consumer countries to cattle raids and organised witchcraft as put forward by the African representatives.

Only later, did I realise that this event represented a common form of knowledge-building or, rather, the organisation of knowledge in

---

[2] In international settings, one does not need much expertise to become a member of an expert group: it is sufficient to be delegated by a state to a meeting. The meeting is then called an "expert meeting", either beforehand or retrospectively. In an EU-meeting about fraud which I attended beginning 1990s, the chairman elevated all the delegates to the status of expert for the elaboration of a point on the agenda, though most had never seen any bookkeeping in their life.

this field of law enforcement. This is not predominantly a matter of solid studies and the thoughtful analysis of hard-discovered data, rather of bringing together important, although not necessarily knowledgeable, people. In general, the more a topic attracts general or political interest, the more important an appropriate organisation of knowledge is. This is the case whether it concerns drug policy (Van Duyne & Levi 2005; Boekhout van Solinge 2000); environmental issues; terrorism (Naylor 2004); or, in our case, "organised crime". However, as with the Interpol meeting, the actual content of this knowledge is only important provided it does not conflict with the prevalent "political mood". The political mood concerning organised crime is that it is a serious matter. Accordingly, a lecture depicting "organised criminals" in all their human banalities meant the undermining of the threat image. That was not the done thing; hence it was considered to be "non-knowledge".[3]

Since 1993 the socio-political organisation of "knowledge" about organised crime was being mobilised. While most knowledge develops through a cyclical process of questioning, answering, falsification and confirmation of that which is the most plausible interpretation until later falsification, the organised crime knowledge development followed the simple but clear path of *confirmation*. One of the most charming statements from the time when the development of "knowledge" began can be found in the proceedings of the UK Organised Crime Conference: "A Threat Assessment", in 1993, of which the first sentence is illustrative: "*Organised crime has many definitions; this may be because it is*

---

[3] Predictably, one will not find such non-knowledge in the mainstream literature like the volume of Fijnaut and Paoli (2004). Nevertheless, the "classic" of Peter Reuter (1983) is just about that criminal disorganised conduct.

like an elephant – it is difficult to describe but you know it when you see it". The elaboration of the spotted organised criminal elephant at the conference did not clarify whether anything "real" was seen at all. However, this did not really matter to either the speaker or the audience. Whatever was put forward at that time and subsequently, it only confirmed what was already believed to be there: "organised crime" *is* there, in whichever animal-like form it may adopt.

It seems that, on the whole, this represents the intellectual baseline from which the "organised crime" knowledge organisation took off at a political level. The next logical step was to go beyond the elephant recognition level, as embodied in the UK document, to search for a common definition. The following step was to make situational descriptions of the phenomenon of "organised crime" based on that definition. Therefore, first, we must examine the definition of organised crime.

Defining organised crime

Defining things is not a popular undertaking: it is considered tedious, pedantic and hair-splitting. It is far easier to say, "I shall know as soon as I see it", rather than sitting down, chewing and ruminating until an unambiguous formula is derived from clear premises. This activity of specifying words and their meanings has to compete with social and cognitive aspects of language use. The ease with which we use words is no guarantee of their precise meaning. As soon as there is some social consensus "that we all understand what we mean" then the urge to determine precise meanings quickly recedes. Accordingly, it is plausible to assume a kind of "social-cognitive saturation": the shared feeling of a diminishing added value with each next analytical step to more sharply delineate meanings of words. This may reduce the analytical efforts for drafting a formula which meets the requirements of an empirical definition: being a precise *decision rule* which assigns an observation x to the delineated set X, or excludes it. Only if this requirement is met, does the definition deserve to be qualified as such. Other, more or less implied requirements are: evidently, the definition should not contain contradictory components (as then it clearly fails as decision rule); nor should it include redundant terms (the demand of "parsimony"). Going through all these requirements is painstaking work, which is not easily reconciled with social-cognitive saturation. What can be observed in the "organised crime" field in this regard?

In each country of the EU, as well as at EU level itself, working groups were formed to elaborate the organised crime definition.[4] Rather predictably, this resulted in as many definitions as there are member states plus the EU definition, coined by the EU working groups.[5] There is no sociological description of the functioning of all these working groups that are tackling the definition problem. We have only the results, analysed in the EU-project "Assessing Organised Crime". The outcome of this analysis (Van Duyne and Van Dijck 2005[6]; 2007), which covered the definitions of Germany, the UK, the Netherlands, Estonia and the 1997 "Enfopol definition" were not encouraging. In terms of penetrating the purported

---
[4] For Germany, see the account by von Lampe (2001).
[5] In 1996 a *High Level Group on Organised Crime* was given the task of drawing up a comprehensive Action Plan. The work of the High Level Group resulted in the *Action Plan of 28 April 1997 to Combat Organised Crime*. This Action Plan set up a *Multidisciplinary Group* (MDG), composed of representatives from the police and the judiciary.
[6] See: www.assessingorganisedcrime.net deliverable 7

essence of "organised crime", a great deal of "retro scholasticism" could be found: medieval thinking around a weird "being" called organised crime (Van Duyne 2003).

None of the definitions analysed met the required standards. The most important flaw in the definitions is that they fail to delineate and cannot therefore act as a decision rule. The simple inclusion of the word "serious" is already lethal due to its lack of analytical clarity: it is a value term unsuitable for inclusion in an empirical definition. Additionally, it does not say anything about the core component: organisation. What is the consequence of the merging of seriousness (or other value terms) with empirical components? It implies the following: while the organisational criminal behaviour (the core meaning) can remain the same, shifting the seriousness threshold determines whether that conduct will be included in the "organised crime" set. Illegal cartel building is a good example. To operate a successful cartel requires a high level of organisation (often an international conspiracy) and well thought-out manipulation of false documents, like invoices, for covering up illegal agreements (Van Duyne 2007). Nevertheless, its (criminal) seriousness is not rated very highly: in most jurisdictions it is an administrative transgression, although pressure is mounting to criminalise illegal cartel building. It could plausibly end up as a form of "organised crime"; while the organisational cheating of the market remains the same.[7] Given the prioritising of the environment, environmental crime may cross the organised crime

---

[7] As a matter of fact, participants in a huge illegal building cartel in the Netherlands have been convicted of taking part in a criminal organisation because of the accompanying criminal offences, such as fraud and corruption. However, the sentences were most lenient: conditional prison sentences and community service.

threshold too, though the ways of organising it remain the same. At present, in practice like in Naples, one needs a mafia involvement for the qualification of organised crime, although the criminal activities remain the same (Massari and Mozini 2004).

After rejecting all definitions which do not delineate, only one definition had stood the test and was left: the definition of the Dutch National Criminal Intelligence Division did delineate properly – by identifying suspect-combinations fulfilling the conditions as counting units. It even objectified "seriousness" by determining a minimum threshold of four years imprisonment for the relevant offences, which in the light of the previous section is debatable, although such a formulation may be a component of an operational definition. However, without even debating the issue, the higher police management did not adopt this definition. Instead they opted for a far weaker, ambiguous definition: one used for a Parliamentary Enquiry in 1995, which was subsequently truncated without giving any clear reason.

Rather than dissecting each national definition and presenting the results as in Van Duyne and Van Dijck (2005), I will only present the analysis of the EU definition, as this is a basic component "instrument" used for the EU threat assessments.

The EU-definition

In its document, ENFOPOL 35, the European Council did not attempt to formulate a precise definition of "organised crime" in one *formal sentence*; instead it listed eleven "characteristics". These were listed in annex IV following the "methodological" (or what was intended to be such) annex. The document does not reveal how these characteristics (or "distinctive features") are to be interpreted or applied. It only specifies that in order for any criminal group to

be classified as "organised crime", at least six characteristics must be present, four of which should be 1, 3, 5 and 11 mentioned below (the mandatory criteria):
1) **Collaboration of more than two people;**
2) each with their own appointed task;
3) **for a prolonged or indefinite period of time** (this criterion refers to the stability and – potential – durability of the group);
4) using some form of discipline or control;
5) **suspected of the commission of serious criminal offences;**
6) operating on an international level;
7) using violence or other means suitable for intimidation.;
8) using commercial or businesslike structures;
9) engaged in money laundering;
10) exerting influence on politics, the media, public administration, judicial authorities or the economy;
11) **motivated by the pursuit of profit and/or power.**

This is a long list in which the mandatory elements are rather dispersed. Actually it resembles a long sentence that has later been split up, after which the obligatory features have been marked. If this "definition" is analytically valid, every component must also be valid. Thus we have to go through the whole list of components. I will simplify this somewhat, by first discussing the mandatory components.

More than two persons (1)
This is a clear bottom line, in agreement with many other national definitions of "organised crime".

For a prolonged or indefinite period of time (this criterion refers to the stability and – potential – durability of the group) (3)

This component falters due to the indeterminate meaning of "prolonged" and "indefinite". Everybody can determine their own time thresholds. According to the Dutch Supreme Court, a time span of just one week was sufficient to qualify the conduct of a cooperation of offenders as "participating in a criminal organisation".[8] Moreover, this criterion says nothing about the temporal "density" of cooperation. Should the collective activities be counted as taking place daily, weekly or at another interval?

Suspected of the commission of serious criminal offences (5)

This is a mixing of facts and values, which can lead to odd outcomes, particularly internationally. I have previously referred to illegal cartel building; in most jurisdictions this is not a criminal offence, but an administrative transgression. Hence it is neither a criminal offence nor "serious". However, the underlying conspiracy and the accompanying documentary fraud can be qualified as "participating in a criminal organisation" in the Netherlands although perhaps not in other jurisdictions. In the UK, this conduct is covered by the conspiracy to defraud; while illegal cartel building is criminalised by the Enterprise Act 2002, as well as the Fraud Act 2006. In a case of cross-border illegal cartel building, the illegal conduct may be qualified as "organised crime" in one jurisdiction but not in another. As remarked earlier, in an empirical definition there is no place for open value terms. For this reason alone, the EU definition fails.

---

[8] HR 16 October 1990, NJ 1991, 442. Though the verdict was criticised for its too liberal conception of the concept of "during considerable time", it demonstrates the defect of a definition with undetermined criteria.

Motivated by the pursuit of profit and/or power (11)

This is an "open door" criterion, which is always fulfilled unless the kinds of crime we are talking about are committed for lust or revenge. As this is not a very likely motive to engage in "organised crime", one may think of the kick or the excitement to be involved in risky business. However, that requires a fair amount of psychological insight in order to determine whether or not the cooperating offenders are just sensation seekers. Therefore we can assume that this condition is always fulfilled, it thereby loses it discriminatory value. Hence, it is simply a "redundant truism" (Kinzig and Luczak 2004).

The intermediate conclusion concerning these mandatory features is: only the first one does not fail the test of ambiguity. The others are unclear or without discriminatory value. Next come the optional features, of which two must be fulfilled in addition to apply the qualification of "organised crime".

Each with their own appointed task (2)

The wording of this condition implies that tasks are assigned by someone, which itself implies a hierarchic structure. The formulation also requires that the appointed tasks are properly described for each of the cooperating criminals. At this juncture, we encounter a practical problem: in the criminal investigative practice, this condition is rarely fulfilled. In many cases that I have studied, only a few of the participants in a criminal "cooperative" had fixed tasks, many were simply factotums, while the role or task of others was unknown. Furthermore, it proves difficult to verify this criterion in cases of criminal network relationships, which are much more frequent (Morselli 2005; Morselli, Gigguere & Petit 2007). Here, applying the concept of "appointed tasks" may fail: in such relationships the connections are too ephemeral and are often changing pragmatically. In short, the wording of this condition implies another organisational principle, while its application fails practically in a large number of cases that are considered "organised crime" too.

Using some form of discipline or control (4)

The wording of this definition is vague: what is "some form"? Moreover, it is not a distinctive feature as it applies to all forms of functional interactions: people working together do exert mutual control and forms of discipline. When it is not a distinctive feature, it must be deleted as redundant.

Operating on an international level (6)

At first sight this is a clear formulation, although an operationalisation is needed for its application. Do we want to include all the criminal connections of a criminal group? In that case, the distinctive value of this feature diminishes, certainly in crime-markets, which are determined by cross-border price differences, and in regions consisting of small jurisdictions, like Europe. What does "international level" mean nowadays in the Schengen area? In addition to this, certain aspects of committing or finalising crime-for-profit are technically almost bound to be cross-border, such as money-laundering or VAT fraud.[9] It is a clear criterion, but from a

---

[9] VAT and excise fraud schemes are also possible within one country, but are less frequent because of the likelihood of early detection. Therefore, most large-scale VAT and excise fraud schemes are cross-border, abusing the destination country principle (Aronowitz et al. 1996). Laundering can also be carried out in one jurisdiction, but as soon as large amounts of money are involved, "inland laundering" becomes a risky affair.

criminal market perspective, it is implied by the international price differences and techniques of committing certain forms of crime. Its discriminatory value is therefore low.

Using violence or other means suitable for intimidation (7)

In the formulation of this condition only the word "violence" clearly covers the use of physical force. The rest of the sentence can imply many sorts of social control and is a consequence of condition 4, to which it should be collated. Hence, it is largely redundant.

Using commercial or businesslike structures (8)

This is an ambiguous formulation as it encompasses abuse as well as normal, neutral use of the commercial aspects of the upperworld, including the criterion of money-laundering below. For this reason, it has a low discriminatory value. It encompasses all economic crime (almost tautologically) and all crimes that require technical handling by an upperworld firm, especially transport in cases of wholesale smuggling (Vander Beken et al. 2005; Von Lampe 2007). In addition, it entails the bulk of the consequential handling of the proceeds (money-laundering). Hence it overlaps with the next feature. Another unresolved question concerns the victimisation of businesses and whether that includes "using" commercial structures?

Engaged in money laundering (9)

This criterion depends on the definition of money laundering. If we apply the all-encompassing definition of the Council of Europe and combine it with the requirement of profit orientation, this condition is always fulfilled. Indeed, as soon as offenders perform any act of hiding or disguising proceeds and so on, they are laundering. As laundering has become the built-in feature of virtually all crimes-for-profit (Van Duyne et al. 2005), it should be considered a redundant criterion: no successful criminal group can avoid it and those who have nothing to launder are not considered "organised crime". Should this feature be maintained, it must become mandatory.

Exerting influence on politics, the media, public administration, judicial authorities or the economy (10)
This is an extremely broad and ambiguous formulation. What is "exerting influence"? If it encompasses all forms of corruption and all levels of public administration, this condition is already fulfilled if smugglers bribe custom officers. It is also fulfilled if a suspect is elected Prime Minister and manipulates Parliament into enacting bills that exonerate his criminal conduct: the case of Berlusconi.

In view of the requirement that, of these optional criteria, two must be fulfilled on top of the first four mandatory, one can conclude this condition is invariably fulfilled as soon as more than two criminals work together (4) and succeed in making money (9), implying some social control and the follow-up money-laundering.

What then remains of this instrument for selecting "organised crime" cases? Only feature (1) survives the test of ambiguity, the other criteria are either unclear, have no or a low discriminating value, overlap or are automatically fulfilled.

This does not look good, certainly not as the basis for EU organised crime statistics (Vettori 2006). Perhaps the definition is, in a rough, unassuming manner, applicable in the reality of law enforcement. To determine this, one should apply it indiscriminately and also to "implausible" targets, such as politicians or high-level corporate crime. Thus, apply all these criteria to Berlusconi, Chirac,

Elf (the corrupt French oil company), erstwhile Chancellor Kohl (carrying around about 30 million DM of party funds) or Parmalat. Indeed, if they all fit the criteria then they should be listed in the Organised Crime Threat Assessment, albeit as an "inconvenient truth". However, they were not!

This definition is the cornerstone of the basic instrument with which the High Level policy-makers in various committees were satisfied. With regard to the underlying social and cognitive processes, one can only speculate. I assume the process of "social and cognitive saturation" set in fairly soon, at least as far as this definition was concerned.

OC situation reports, dissatisfaction and move to threat assessments

In November 1993, the European Council decided that an annual strategic report on organised crime was to be issued. The aim of this report would be to provide insight into the organised crime phenomenon within the European Union. In November 1994, the Council accepted that the production of this *Organised Crime Situation Report* (OCSR) depended upon the exchange and analysis of information by the member states. All of those involved in drafting OC situation reports (nationally as well as on the EU-level) appeared to accept the strange ENFOPOL definition. Nevertheless, there was a keen awareness of the defects in the OC situation reports: the "Crimorg" documents (a shorthand for the organised crime documents) reflect a continuous desire for improvement, expressed by the "experts" and subsequently by the Council of Ministers (Vander Beken 2003). All those involved realised that the key weakness of the EU Organised Situation Report were attributable to data collection at the national level (Vettori 2006). This was also regularly expressed in various "CRIMORG-documents". Therefore, the recommendation concerning the harmonisation of data collection by the member states repeatedly appears. Although this is quite an obvious requirement, the repetition of this recommendation demonstrated that this defect was (and is) not yet resolved.

We are not informed about the way in which such EU OC-situation reports were composed. As the OC-reports were deduced from the national OC situation reports, we must turn to these underlying documents. In the framework of the EU project *Assessing Organised Crime*, the Tilburg University project partners analysed the situation reports of the UK, Germany, the Netherlands and Belgium. This analysis showed that they were unsuitable to provide the basis for any EU OC situation report.

Firstly, they varied enormously in their methodology. In this respect, the basic foundation is essential: the definition which is the decision rule for data collection. These – national – definitions once more reveal serious flaws and are unfit to be used as a data collection decision rules. Furthermore, even if the definition would be analytically valid, its concrete application is not stipulated. We have the impression that, although a definition was mentioned at the beginning of a report, nobody heeded this in the subsequent text. That which the local OC detective squads had in their investigation or intelligence basket was considered to be OC, irrespective of any definition.

Secondly, from no situation report can the reader deduce at which level of investigation the data were collected. "Soft" and hard data, both are without differentiation mixed in the description. In a rather careless manner, the reports fail to account for the ways in which the various levels of observation contribute to the situation description. As with the UK OC threat assessment 2003 or 2006/7, it is simply "stock taking" of absolutely anything put side by side indiscriminately and pasted together within one picture.[10] Which data have been validated and how? It is of little help much to counter that valid data are hard to get, so those writing the reports have to resort to "unsubstantiated intelligence" (the assembly of "what may-be": facts, fiction or faction) and subsequently present all of this in the guise of a this-it-is description.

Thirdly, there is a general lack of accountability in the entire assessment process, from data collection to the results of the analysis and their conversion into a descriptive narrative with conclusions or recommendations that are, at times, far reaching. There is no presentation of an interlocking chain from basic observations to outcomes, nor is there a step-by-step "reasoning path" enabling cognitive checking. Every attempt to penetrate "the making-of" in order to check it is arrested by invoking the "confidentiality" and "safety" arguments.

Eventually, the results of these uncontrollable and ill-designed national situation descriptions arrive at EUROPOL in order to be converted into an EU OC report. The ways in which this is accomplished remain, once more, hidden; there is no account of the "making-of" either here. Of course, the OC description (OCR) is presented as produced under the umbrella of the ENFOPOL definition, which is not true. Not all Member States use this definition and of those who say they do, its mode of application is uncertain, given the multi-interpretable criteria (Vander Beken

---

[10] *UK threat assessment. The threat from serious and organised crime 2003.* National Criminal Intelligence Service. *The United Kingdom threat assessment of serious organised crime 2006/7.* SOCA.

2004). This definition is simply superimposed on whatever Europol recieves into its mail.

We do not know whether, or in which way, the OCRs have been formally evaluated, as there are no records of this. At any rate, in various years there were signs that dissatisfaction had set in. In 1997, guidelines were proposed, which among others included the ENFOPOL definition analysed above. In 1999, the German presidency made proposals to improve the procedure, albeit heavily based on the manner in which the German OC situation reports were produced.[11] The proposals emphasised the need for harmonisation and uniform collection of data, although these were based on the guidelines of 1997, which continued the – unworkable – basis. It also suggested the use of a broader range of socio-political and economic data in order to produce a threat assessment. The dissatisfaction concerned not only the sordid methodology, but particularly the difficulties with any practical application of the OCR. When these proposals failed to evoke much activity, the Swedish delegation took up the same thread in 1999–2000 and made additional proposals for improvement with the aim of *strategic* planning. Precisely what this strategic planning is supposed to be is not explained; at any rate it was, however, related to prioritising and common actions. However, who is to prioritise in Europe in organised crime matters and in what way common actions are to be deployed, remains unclear.

The general direction had become clear: fanned by the Belgian delegation in the committees, there was dissatisfaction with situation reports and a clear move towards a *threat* assessment of

---

[11] Council of the European Union, 8469/99, CRIMORG 55, Brussels, 19th May 1999.

organised crime and *future* oriented reports.[12] This presupposed a "developing of a strategic concept on tackling organised crime".[13] In the same year, on the 2nd June 2005, the Commission issued a specific communication to the Council and EU Parliament in which it proposed the development of a European Criminal Intelligence Model (ECIM), the key element of which should be a European OC threat assessment (OCTA) by Europol.[14] In October 2005, the Council took the last step: it determined that from 1st January 2006 onwards, Europol was to produce an Organised Crime Threat Assessment (OCTA), replacing its annual Organised Crime Situation Reports.[15] As was stated earlier, this should be essential for the development of a common intelligence model by Europol and the Member States. For the first time, Europol was to be allowed to put its own interpretative work into the assessment rather than simply reflecting the variable analysis of individual Member States contributions.

Meanwhile, throughout all these years of talking about a harmonised methodology and so forth, none of the methodological basic

---

[12] Council of the European Union, 14959/1/01, CRIMORG 133, Brussels, 10th December 2001.

[13] Communication from the Commission to the Council and the European Parliament, The Hague Programme: ten priorities for the next five years. The partnership for European renewal in the field of freedom, security and justice, OJC 236, 24th September 2005.

[14] Communication from the Commission to the Council and the European Parliament, COM(2005)232 final, Developing a strategic concept on tackling organised crime, 2nd June 2005; Council of the European Union, 9778/2/05, Council and Commission Action Plan implementing the Hague Programme on strengthening freedom, security and justice in the European Union, 10th June 2005.

[15] Council of the European Union, 10180/4/05, Council conclusions on intelligence-led policing and the development of the Organised Crime Threat Assessment (OCTA), 3rd October 2005.

requirements had been met. A cursory stock-take in CRIMORG yields the plausible conclusion that none of the Member States heeded guidelines or calls for harmonisation. Indeed, the method of data collection of some Member States is even unknown; while for others, there are only vague indications of a "methodology", which are sufficient to arouse fears of the methodological worst-case scenario. Admittedly, the whole methodological package sent to the Member States by the Multi Disciplinary Group or other High Level experts, looked extremely amateurish too. Moreover, its basis, the ramshackle definition, was never debated or reconsidered. Hence, while the Council, the Commission and "expert" committees pronounced lofty words about the "future looking" OCTAs, the methodological and underlying equipment were virtually absent. Nevertheless, there was a dim awareness that some bits and pieces of the methodology must also be improved, therefore a new questionnaire was to be designed. This will be discussed later.

OCTA! The big unaccountable promise

Finally, in the autumn of 2006, the first OCTA was launched, soon followed by the 2007 OCTA. In both cases, the director was "delighted to present [...] it [as] a core product of the intelligence led policing concept and its drafting is one of Europol's top priorities...." To the reader, this sounds like a big promise, although the public version is, of course, stripped of all information which may jeopardize investigatory interests. Nevertheless, the public version must still reflect this "intelligence led policing" and the "forward looking" approach which should render the OCTA so very different from the ordinary OC situation reports. What, then, can be deduced from these OCTAs? I have reviewed OCTA 2006

(Trends in Organised Crime 2007), from which I have taken those points that are also relevant for OCTA 2007. The most important aspect is the point of *accountability*. In both, OCTAs the reader is fobbed off with fine statements such as:

> The OCTA is based on a multi-source approach, including law enforcement and non-law enforcement sources. These sources include various European agencies as well as the private sector. A specific emphasis is put on elaborating the benefits of an intensified public-private partnership.

However, at no point in the two OCTAs is one single line devoted to questions such as the nature of the basic input resulting from this "multi source approach". There is no reference to notions of reliability, validity or comparability. Again, the question of the definition was not raised: was the multi-source approach based on a multi-source definition? Granted, leaving the definition unchanged imparted peace and rest (no new definition debate!), but it is far from certain that multi-source data collection was based on the ENFOPOL definition. Actually, even if the same definition is adopted but applied differently due to a lack of operationalisation then there will be different outcomes. No single line is devoted to this possibility. Given the invalidity of the ENFOPOL definition, one may consider this an aggravation of an existing flaw.

Of course, the OCTAs are about threats. Accordingly, the reader is eager to find out which kinds of organised crime dangers will cross his path, in the near future at least. The most frequently mentioned threat category appears to come from the non-indigenous crime-groups. In both reports, they are referred to most frequently: 16 times in 2006, and 10 times in 2007.

In conclusion, the situation where a non-indigenous criminal group resorts to international operations and also aims at managing the distribution phase within the EU markets is the highest threat.

(OCTA 2006, 6)

However, within a year, OCTA 2007 discovers a new threat related to the non-indigenous criminals: the second generation! In OCTA 2006, the phrase "second generation" does not appear once; in 2007 it appears seven times. Non-indigenous crime groups appear to be dangerously assimilating (or integrating) into the EU host countries, which should certainly be considered a new threat. Apparently the authors of OCTA 2006 (and the police units filling the underlying questionnaire) were lacking in both contemporary and older literature about criminal organisations integrating ethnic minorities (Kleemans et. al. 2002). The 2007 OCTA provides no account of this sudden discovery.

Another frequently recurring threat is the reference to the (ab)use of *legitimate business structures*: in 2006 there are seven references; in 2007 this number increases to twenty-four. What has changed and what is the "future-orientedness" of this threat? The connection to VAT fraud (mentioned once in 2006 and five times in 2007) is certainly not new and is very obvious (try to get your VAT back without a registered firm). Since 1993, cross-border VAT fraud has increased due to the introduction of the destination principle. Due to the open borders, on-the-spot border control was replaced by more remote invoice control. Actually, this was the widening of the existing – highly fraud sensitive – VAT regime in the Benelux countries to the other EU countries (Van Duyne 1991; Aronowitz et. al. 1996; EU Commission 1998). A very long running and ongoing threat indeed. Other connections to legitimate business or to being a part of such business structures are also fairly evident and quite well established. Large-scale criminal operations, usually concerning transport, have typically been executed by means of registered transport firm, which is a traditionally vulnerable sector (Vander Beken et al. 2005).

When reading and re-reading the two OCTAs, one searches in vain for that promised future-orientedness. Apparently the authors, the High Level committees, the Council or the Commission did not apply the equivalent of a "Wikipedia" test: What can we learn about criminal threats by simply typing in all the search words of the OCTAs in Wikipedia?

This outcome raised some curiosity about the "making-of" the OCTAs: what were the processes, analysis and "reasoning paths" from the raw data input to this output? What does the basic instrument – the questionnaire – look like? I tried to find the answers to these questions.

Knock, Knock

Inspection of the methodology begins with the research tools, which, in many research projects, comprise a questionnaire; this is also the case with OCTA. Therefore, in January 2007, I requested that Europol management reveal their methodology concerning OCTA 2006 and hand over their *empty* questionnaire. In a long-winded letter, the responsible manager replied that handing over this document would be difficult as that would require the consent of *all* the member states. He did not refer to the treaty text upon which this response was based, nor whether any action could be taken to comply with my request. The response did not contain a decision, only that complying with my request was "difficult".

As the Dutch police received the Europol questionnaire for its contribution to the yearly OCTA and as it had thereby become a Dutch document, I requested that the competent authority, the Minister of Justice, hand over that document and all the other documents related to the threat assessment methodology under the Dutch Freedom of Information Act.[16] The Ministry of Justice (the Secretary-General) refused my request as "it could disturb relations with Europol due to ignoring its decision" and "because it may jeopardise ongoing investigations".

The motivation of this refusal was wrong: Europol did not make any decision, but only stated that "it would be difficult"; and in no way could it be justified that seeing an *empty* questionnaire could endanger police operations. The reasons given were therefore defective, which is grounds for launching a complaint against the ministry with the following basic arguments:
- No policy report without public justification;
- This is an empirical assessment of an important public issue; hence the public must be able to determine the validity of such a policy report;
- If a public body is allowed to hide an *empty* questionnaire, which other important things will it be allowed to hide from public scrutiny?

---

[16] Wet Openbaarheid van Bestuur (WOB).

- A methodology is about formal procedures of fact-finding and formal deductions and must not cover confidential contents.[17] This part of the justification fails because of a clear lack of professional understanding;
- Europol must express its displeasure at the prospect of the Minister handing over the empty questionnaire in writing and with a proper justification. If the Minister accepts Europol's stand then Europol's (defects of) justification will become that of the Minister;
- I will appeal to the Administrative Court against such a decision, as well as against any non-disclosure of future OCTA methodologies.

Meanwhile the Socialist Party, concerned about the (lack of) democratic responsibility of Europol (to whom is it really accountable?) asked questions about the OCTA accountability in the Dutch Second Chamber. In the European Parliament, I prompted the Dutch Socialist representative to ask similar questions. While the EP representative was rebuffed with an almost blunt answer[18], the Dutch Minister of Justice agreed with the point regarding lack of democratic responsibility and put this issue on the agenda of

---

[17] One of the Italian colleagues is of the opinion that the methodology is an aspect of the confidential parts of the report to be included in the "closed version". Discussing the methodology with Europol would be instructive, but to whom if the discussion remains behind "closed doors"?

[18] Paraphrased: It is at Europol's discretion to determine whether, or for which reasons, questionnaires or other methodological aspects may jeopardize state security or the efforts to fight organised crime. Europol can act without the approval of the Council of Ministers. Europol documents are not submitted to the Council. So who is accountable for Europol's "common agreed-upon methodology"? Not the Council, nor the Board of Supervisors, which only supervises.

the Board of Supervisors of Europol. Surprisingly, he was met with "open ears" among the represented Member States. I was told that *all but one* Member States were willing to have the OCTA methodology disclosed, the exception being Italy.

The official hearing took place in October 2007 and the Hearing Committee drew up a positive advice to the Minister who had to decide *personally*: he could not delegate the decision to one of his top civil servants, e.g. his Secretary General. As was expected following the Minister's initiative in the Board of Supervisors, he decided positively and handed over the requested documents, leaving Europol fuming for a while.[19] At the time of writing, it appeared that Europol has appealed against the decision of the Minister, which in the meantime cannot be undone: the documents have already been handed over.

What of Academia? Earlier, I sent all of those involved in organised crime research an e-mail, explaining my stance and inviting them to support me by initiating a similar national Information of Freedom procedure. What was the outcome?

- From the UK there was no response;
- Of the three addressed German organised crime experts, one took action and addressed a Member of the Bundestag;
- Two more countries responded, but the respondents explained that although they agreed with my stance, they have such a good relationship with Europol that they were not in a position to submit any formal request. Moreover, they "could already get all the information we wanted" (although therefore cannot use it). OK, these are the "embedded researchers".

---

[19] One of our daily newspapers, *NRC/Handelsblad*, launched a similar request and also followed a formal Freedom of Information procedure (thus, there may have been two lawsuits with proper publicity).

It is cause for celebration that there are so many criminologists who will guarantee intellectual continuity by *not* perishing on the barricades in case democratic principles really are "under fire".

The instruments

The questionnaires used for OCTA 2006 and OCTA 2007 are very different instruments and this negates any comparison of outcomes. How should one evaluate these newly designed instruments? Of course, the only criterion is the objective of the exercise itself: a valid representation of the threat of "organised crime". Moreover, this depends on the ways in which the basic concepts in the questionnaires are defined: flaws in the definitions or no definition at all contribute to uncertainties and ambiguities in the answers. As these answers come from 27 member states, one can project the degree of cumulative ambiguity in the final outcomes, which must then be multiplied by two, given the incomparability of the two instruments. I shall therefore discuss them separately.

a) OCTA 2006

The introductory section to this questionnaire opens with some confusion. The keywords, threat and risk, are not really properly defined. The same applies to their relationship. The very short, haltingly formulated sections can hardly be considered clarifying texts with a conceptual analysis, followed by a proper delineation of the key concepts. The only things we are told is that "the purpose of threat assessment is to analyse the character, scope and impact of criminality". We are also informed that it "will be long term, future oriented and therefore have the most difficult level of analytical ambition" (p 7). This looks like a tempering of expectations. In a later section (4.1) this is repeated by stating that a new methodology will only provide a rough estimate.

The two other introductory sections indicate correctly that organised crime should be projected against the landscape of Political, Economic, Social, Technological, Environmental and Legislative circumstances. These constitute the so-called PEST(EL) analysis (See also Vander Beken 2005). As direct measurement of the impact/threat of OC is not possible, indirect measures must be developed from existing indicators. These indicators "should enable the analysts to describe the potential Strength, Weakness, Opportunity and Threats (SWOT analysis) as basic ingredients of the Threat Assessment, with respect to OC groups involved". Note that in the SWOT analysis to assess threat as an *outcome* variable, "threat" also functions as a descriptive *input* variable. In the very short text, there is apparently no space for such subtleties – the following pages of the document deal with the 27 indicator-questions concerning "criminal groups active in OC".[20]

The 27 questions convey a strange and amateurish impression. They have to be answered for each detected crime-group, added together and then analysed collectively. Exactly how that is to be accomplished remains a mystery. Some questions are factual, for example those about group size[21]; others ask clearly for an *opinion* such as: "Was the group forced to change tactics?" or "Were you able to disrupt the activities of the group?" Another

---

[20] "Active in OC": a strange and awkward formulation when "organised crime" is defined in terms of characteristics *and* activities of the criminal group.

[21] Strangely enough, the answers are already categorised in intervals instead of exact numbers. For example, not "active since [year]" but "active for: 0–1; 1–3 years" and so forth. The same applies for the number of group members. This results in an avoidable loss of statistical information.

question appears to be tautological: "Disrupting the activities of the group shows an impact on the group activities?" or overlap with the following question. Some questions are ambiguous, for example, "Does the group have several branches, being responsible for different tasks (distribution of responsibilities)?" This question resembles the second criterion of "organised crime": "each [member] with their own appointed task", which implies "a distribution of responsibilities". A few questions are likely to evoke a "correct response": "The group activities are of concern to the public?" Given that we are dealing with "serious" crime, it would be strange if the answer would be "no", certainly not if by "concern to the public", *media attention* is meant. As the police are an important actor for steering the media then, to a considerable degree, public concern reflects police media policy.[22]

After these OC indicator-questions concerning criminal groups that are "active in OC", the questionnaire continues with nine "crime type related questions". These are open questions, with the exception of the last one. Some of these questions can only be answered if the police officer/respondent is prepared to write a lengthy essay about the development of criminal landscape *per crime type*: increase/decrease, victims, changes in legislation or priority setting. The respondents are then asked to write about their opinion of differences with other developments and which developments they expect in the coming year. Subsequently, the respondents are asked to provide an estimate of OC involvement in the type of crime described (they are asked to give a rough estimate as a percentage; yet how is one supposed to do that?).

---

[22] Of course, there are forms of "organised crime" which may hardly be of concern to "the public": e.g. cigarette smuggling or VAT fraud despite media attention.

The majority of the questions are accompanied by explanatory notes, some of which add to rather than reduce confusion. It is of very little help if the explanatory note details that the question concerns a "subjective judgement".

One must keep in mind that twenty-seven national police agencies have to respond to this confusing questionnaire, which is bound to result in twenty-seven equally confusing response sheets.

b) OCTA 2007

The questionnaire of the 2007 OCTA has a different format to its predecessor. The questions are more detailed and also better formulated, although no easier to answer. This opacity is in spite of around fifty explanatory footnotes, which far exceed the quantity and length of the thirty-three questions. Some questions assume broad general knowledge. For example, respondents are required to answer questions about the relevant environment while paying attention to "the level of taxation, political or economic situation in certain non-EU countries, historical and cultural links with certain non-EU countries, geographical position, etc." Should such general knowledge be lacking (this is quite likely) then respondents would be compelled to spend a considerable amount of time consulting Wikipedia, for example.

Aside from the ambiguous ENFOPOL definition, stipulated in the preamble, ambiguities slip in at other places too. For example, mentioning "serious or organised crime" (which is it: serious, organised or both?) and references to "syndicates" in the explanatory footnote to the first question. Some questions are token examples of fuzzy thinking, embarrassing and burdening the officers. Examples include questions about "growth potential" of a criminal group (or syndicate?), or the "cohesion factor", which virtually invite respondents to compose a sociological essay on each crime-group or crime type. A few "clarifying" footnotes also prompt the respondent to particular answers, a capital crime in methodology. This is examplified by the footnotes to question 12 (of which there are three) pertaining to the influence of legal business structures on the market. Asking to "specify" the footnote provides a lengthy exposé on the perverse effects of legal persons in the hands of criminals. In such a manner, the answer is virtually prompted. The same occurs with questions concerning criminal cooperation or corruption.

The questions about the criminal activities open with the announcement that "whenever the question refers to specific figure[s], the question is not restricted to factual information". The second sentence makes it clear that this non-factual information may be "intelligence" and "therefore may not currently be substantiated by available evidence". Apart from its value for investigative purposes, intelligence in this almost "non-factual" way is likely to produce answers of fiction or at best "faction" and of questionable reliability.[23]

After 18 questions about criminal groups (or syndicates) and 14 questions about criminal activities (with a great deal of overlap), all concerning what is being observed (including the intelligence faction modus) *at present*, the questionnaire ends with the sole future oriented question: "Please provide a future oriented assessment concerning changes in this criminal activity" (that is: for each

---

[23] There is a thick conceptual fog surrounding "intelligence". It should be something with the form of "soft" information, but what is "soft"? This can range from the infamous hunches of undercover police officers, gossip and also to factual observations that cannot be disclosed – as doing so would endanger the lives of (criminal) informants.

described criminal activity). There are no guidelines detailing how to use the observations presented in the earlier answers in order to draft a future oriented assessment.

Given the nature of these instruments it was to be expected that they produced outcomes that were difficult to interpret. Likewise, the interpretative models of PEST and SWOT elaborated in OCTA 2006, do not deliver: Were they intended to elicit the respondents' interpretation – and if so how? Alternatively, were these models intended for the analysis by Europol? We do not know because after being mentioned once their use remains obscure. How this instrument could have resulted in the OCTA 2006 and 2007 should indeed be considered an admirable piece of magic art! The logical conclusion is that these questionnaires should never have been presented to any respondent in the police forces of the Member States in the first place.

Do these two questionnaires constitute the entire instrument? No, they do not: an instrument does not merely consist of a visible tool, like a thermometer, it also is accompanied by instructions for its use. An improperly used instrument leads to false observations. In this case, the completed questionnaires (Europol's observations) without instructions for their subsequent analysis and further interpretation lead to unaccountable selectivity. Hence, the pertinent question is: How has the data that constitutes the raw input of the 27 responding states been converted into the amalgamated pictures of the two OCTAs? Unfortunately, this aspect of the instrument remains hidden (if it indeed exists at all) as it is not a part of the documents requested under the Dutch Freedom of Information Act. Of course, the issue of whether Europol really possesses such methodological instructions for input processing is most intriguing: there should be at least *a written protocol, its use supervised and accounted for in writing.* Compare this with the conditions in public health research, if an assessment of "Asian flu" had been conducted without proper research protocol (or definition) then heads would have rolled. As there are no indications that Europol has such a protocol or – in the event that one does exist – no account of its use is provided, we are forced to determine the reliability and validity of the OCTAs from the questionnaires themselves (including the definition). These are sufficiently defective to deny the OCTAs any credibility.

The organisation of (OC) knowledge re-assessed

This overview of the organisation of OC knowledge concerning threats may puzzle the reader (as it did the author). Where is the evidence of evidence-based policy making? Moreover, can OCTA evidence be found that transcends the Wikipedia level? Should there be no evidence of either points then we must address another question: How could such a large organisation of knowledge-building, representing 27 Member States and encompassing High Level and Multi-disciplinary groups plus informal working groups of "experts", yield such poor results? Is this outcome attributable to the "socio-cognitive saturation"? This may have played a role in the phase of defining "organised crime" (itself a tedious job). It may have also been instrumental in the decision-making process leading to the change from the unsatisfactory situation reports to threat assessments. There was already a great deal of talk and pressure from various Member States – among them Belgium – to the effect that something must be changed (Vander Beken 2004). Indeed, when the political time was ripe, things changed.

However, this may not have been the only influencing factor. Judging from documentation, trusted police phrases, particularly the phrase "pro-active" may have played a leading role in shaping a mindset which predisposed a similar design: a "future oriented" strategic instrument. In principle, there is nothing wrong with this idea. However, the present setting for the development of such an instrument is an uncontrollable multi-country, ill-standardised police environment, which is dealing with a poorly defined phenomenon. Accordingly, an exhaustively painstaking and time-consuming, methodological preparation by professionals is demanded. These conditions were not fulfilled. Without such professionalism the entire concept of a "pro-active" instrument with amalgamated unsorted, non-standardised data intended to provide input at strategic level is little more than wishful thinking. Indeed, the OCTA approach was steered by well-meaning police amateurs[24] who were in turn advising even more amateurish high-level policy-makers. In addition, the policy makers were in a hurry: "Something had to be done" . . . and soon!

Within this context of time-pressure and socio-cognitive saturation, the preparation was bound to remain analytically shallow. During my participation in a preparatory group, I noticed that deeper (re-)analysis had been eschewed ("We have already gone through that"; "that has already been accepted"; "we have no time to re-open that debate because we have deadlines") At the same time, a dialogue with academic outsiders was thin and biased towards confirmation. Although critical ideas were listened to politely, no response was forthcoming. It is of little surprise then, that

---

[24] There were a few professionals present in the preparatory informal meetings but the documents reveal no trace of their input.

we subsequently find neither sharp analysis nor a solid foundation for following the "pro-active" and "future oriented" course. The wording sound impressive, so who dares to be a detractor?

In contrast to this decision path, some documents reflect a keen awareness that there were a great many methodological obstacles; the most important of these was the lack of standardised data collection. Time and time again, this has been mentioned in the CRIMORG papers. However, this worry was overruled by pressure from above insisting that something-must-be-done.

I believe we have arrived at the major flaw in the whole enterprise: the attempt to organise knowledge in a political setting in which the political element dominates. This led to decision-making and project execution under adverse political pressure, which thereby did not permit any re-thinking. Once a decision was made and its outcome was included in a policy paper, it became difficult to reverse it. This context conflicts with one of the basic features of knowledge: it is always reversible. To further aggravate this context, it is also affected by an inward-looking *police* culture of secrecy, illustrated by the refusal to disclose the empty questionnaire. Under such conditions, it was irresponsible to start such an ambiguous knowledge project as OCTA; particularly when highly ponderous counter-indications have been explicitly cited. In normal research settings, such a decision would never have been allowed. To return to the question of the introduction: the standards for a proper organisation of knowledge were not met.

Should the police have abstained entirely from drafting a threat assessment in the first place? The answer is a simple "yes": the organisation of knowledge in order to draft a valid threat assessment is not a police matter, either within the police organisation directly or indirectly, under its guidance (and pressure). Organising knowledge pertaining to public safety (OC threat) needs a corresponding environment in which the standards of independence, transparency and accountability are taken seriously. The responsibility of such an undertaking concerns issues of reliability and validity. This differs from the responsibility of maintaining safety of law enforcement. Creating knowledge about threats to safety should not be the task of the agency that also has the task of maintaining safety: that implies a high potential of conflict of interest. Compare this with a corporation and a security firm. Should the management of the corporation feel comfortable if it orders the drafting of a risk assessment from a security firm with prior knowledge that it would also be tasked to work with its own assessments and recommendations? It would, of course, have a vested interest in all sorts of (big) threats. As a matter of fact, such a situation would be contrary to the EU regulation for tendering projects: the firm that draws up the terms of reference of a project will never be invited for the subsequent tender. As the EU acts so responsibly in tendering procedures, it should be even more sensitive and responsible when it concerns safety: drafting OCTAs is not a police task.

Clearly, "something has to be done". We can make repairs within the present framework, as proposed by Vettori (2006). I am of the opinion that this approach would result in a patchwork approach with stopgaps. The alternative harm-risk assessment, already proposed by Vander Beken (2003) still hinges on the old *a priori* definition and on even more interpretational dilemmas.[25] Instead, we need a new approach and another organisation of

---

[25] Though a risk model seems attractive, as soon as the number of interacting concepts increase, the definitional problems increase commensurate: "intentions", "capabilities", "expectations" are difficult to operationalise. See Vander Beken (2004).

knowledge concerning "organised crime", one befitting the standards of knowledge.

A way out: a New European Common Approach[26]

The last sentence of the previous section appears to slam the door to drafting OCTAs. This is not correct. Another approach is feasible should we be prepared to retrace our steps and return to the basics of empirical referents and reliable and valid data (Von Lampe 2004a; 2004b). If we recognise that "organised crime" is just a construction rather than an observation then a question presents itself: What is being observed? The answer is simple: perpetrators offending for money. This basic angle entails that the *counting unit* at the observational level will be the conduct of the individual: *Who does what*? Naturally, the next variable will be: *With whom*? This implies an important first shift:

- from "criminal groups" – also a construct – to criminal conduct and to the individuals involved in those activities.

This provides the first essential *counting units*, which are lacking in the OCTAs. Collecting data at this elementary level implies a shift from lay-theory led "organised crime" assessments to empirically grounded theory building. In short, at this level the phrase "organised crime" is simply not mentioned, although the "with whom" variable entails the "organising variable" as a form of conduct, albeit as a dependent variable rather than as an axiom. Criminal conduct *being organised*.

---

[26] See: Assessing organised crime by a New Common European approach. Final report. www.assessingorganisedcrime.net

Of course, that more general principle is far from yielding an assessment. Hence, the next question is whether we must convert that principle into a new instrument to replace the work done for the Europol OCTA? The simple answer is: no new instrument but a new approach using the existing tools! Nothing *extra* should be designed, nor should questionnaires be issued to be completed retrospectively. Instead, the existing paperwork should be integrated with the raw data input, inserting *while* doing the normal detective work. This entails the job of reporting observations and registering being virtually the *same* act, which will result in a data document (an electronic one). In concrete terms, after writing the text of his protocol (which is basically a narrating series of statements), the detective must give a preformatted summary consisting of the relevant variables. The first skeleton data entry functions as a kind of summary document that stays with the case, rather like a bill of lading (delivery note) accompanies cargo. This "criminal bill of lading" will be fed into the database for later statistical analysis and overviews. Summarized, this approach means:

- that observing and registering will be virtually the *same* act, which results in a document (electronic) that (if a criminal case is made) "travels" with the case, like a bill of lading travels with the cargo;
- and that, at every stage in the "journey" through the judicial system, data can be added, deleted or changed while the officer in charge is at close observational range;
- At every stage, a copy of this document will be inserted into the criminal database.

Data thus gathered are the quantitative backbone for assessing crime-for-profit, more accurately: criminal *conduct* by profit-oriented *offenders* including the variable of co-offending. However, where does "organised crime" come in? Indeed, is that phrase necessary in this phase of data collection? What added value or explanatory function does the concept of "organise crime" have? As it is a political construction, it does not belong at the level of fact-collecting data input. This level, the "*raw data level*" (level 1) must be "brand free": *no label* attached. This is in order to prevent the "Columbus effect": Columbus set out to detect India, so he sailed in pursuit of this objective and indeed did return with Indians. The same happens with the OCTAs: send out questionnaires with the heading "organised crime" and everything you receive will be labelled indiscriminately as such. As recipient, Europol is not in a position to conduct tests of falsification to rectify this undifferentiated input (nor to disclose publicly how it contends with that).

Given that we obtain a more reliable and ongoing data input, the agencies run the risk of being swamped by data. To prevent this, the activities at the *statistical analysis level* (level 2) begin by applying filters and thresholds that are considered relevant. Are these derived from some general "organised crime" definition? No, because a variety of thresholds may have to be used. For organised burglary, the financial threshold may be much lower than for the organisation of cigarette smuggling or VAT fraud. Of course, setting thresholds implies making cut-off lines within a population, which must be accounted for, particularly if different cut-off lines are to be used. Such decisions can be empirically justified, given the heterogeneity of the criminal populations that make up the total set. For example, cigarette smugglers (or VAT organisers) are rarely found in the drugs markets and vice versa (Van Dijck, 2007). The differences between these populations justify different thresholds.

The statistical processing should develop into a standard routine, producing regularly overviews of the criminal landscape. The outcome of such analyses will be the input for in-depth investigations using qualitative methods also: interviews, open sources and criminal files. At this third level, the analysis goes beyond a stocktake or description of offenders, offences or structures, it will also include environmental variables concerning legal, social, economic and cultural conditions that interact with the criminal players. (The reader may recognise the PEST variable, this time properly accounted for). This does not necessarily entail a society-broad unwieldy approach, as the selection of such variables depends on the particular research questions to be addressed.

Information concerning the other three levels of data-processing and analysis may be input at the level of scientific research (level 4). At this level, researchers can focus on formulating theories and testing hypotheses concerning particular phenomena. It should be noted that empirically based theory building does not necessarily lead to a "comprehensive organised crime theory", which is unlikely to exist should there be no homogeneous "organised crime population".

The research level is also the proper place for some reflexive work on the agencies involved as "organised crime" does not stand alone: it is connected to all the law enforcement agencies, policy-making and legislation, which form the cornerstone of the crime-markets. Researching the organisation of crime should be complemented by critically researching the *faits et gestes* of these agencies and legislators. Indeed, if profit oriented criminals are interesting, so are their crime-fighters and their mutual interactions.

In the end the reader may wonder whether "organised crime" has silently slipped away. I do not think so: it remains a phrase for exciting conversations, political discourse and policy making, and – if no changes are made – keeps police officers busy with organised crime assessments.

References

Aronowitz A.A., D.C.G. Laagland & G. Paulides 1996. *Value-added Tax fraud in the European Union*. Amsterdam, Kugler Publications

Boekhout van Solinge, T. 2000. *De besluitvorming rond drugs in de Europese Unie*. Amsterdam, CEDRO/Mets en Schilt

Dijck, M. van 2000. "Cigarette shuffle : organising tobacco tax evasion in the Netherlands". Duyne, P.C. van, A. Maljevic, M. van Dijck, K. von Lampe & J. Harvey eds.: *Crime business and crime-money in Europe : The dirty linen of illicit enterprise*. Nijmegen, Wolf Legal Publishers

Duyne, P.C. van 1991. "Crime-enterprises and the legitimate industry". Fijnaut, C. and J. Jacobs eds.: *Organized crime and its containment : A transatlantic initiative*. Deventer, Kluwer Law and Taxation Publishers

Duyne, P.C. van 2000. "Mobsters are human too : behavioural science and organised crime investigation". *Crime, Law and Social Change* 34. 369–390

Duyne, P.C. van 2003. "Medieval thinking and organized crime economy". Viano, E., J. Magallanes and L. Bridel eds.: *International organized crime : myth, power and profit*. Anderson Publishing

Duyne, P.C. van 2007. "OCTA 2006 : the unfulfilled promise". *Trends in Organized Crime* 3. 120–128

Duyne, P.C. van 2007. "All in the Dutch construction family : cartel building and organised crime". L. Holmes ed.: *Terrorism, organised crime and corruption : networks and linkages*. Cheltenham, Edward Elgar

Duyne, P.C. van, & M. van Dijck 2007. "Assessing organised crime : the sad state of an impossible art". Bovenkerk, F. and M. Levi eds.: *The organised crime economy : Essays in honor of Alan Block*. New York, Springer

Duyne, P.C. van, M.S. Groenhuijsen & A.A.P. Schudelaro 2005. "Balancing financial threats and legal interests in money-laundering policy". *Crime, Law and Social Change* 43. 117-147

Duyne, P.C. van, R. Kouwenberg & G. Romeijn 1990. *Misdaadondernemingen : Ondernemende misdadigers in Nederland*. Arnhem, Gouda-Quint

Duyne, P.C. van & M. Levi 2005. *Drugs and money : Managing the drug trade and crime-money in Europe*. London, Routledge

Duyne, P.C. van, M. Pheijffer, H.G. Kuijl, Th.H. van Dijk & G. Bakker 2003. *Financial Investigation of Crime : A tool of the integral law enforcement approach*. Nijmegen, Wolf Legal Publishers

European Commission 1998. *Special report No 9/98 on the protection of the European Union's financial interests in the field of VAT on intra-Community trade and the response of the Commission*. Brussels, European Comission

Kinzig, J. & A. Luczak 2004. "Organised crime in Germany : a passé-partout definition encompassing different phenomena". Fijnaut, C. and L. Paoli eds.: *Organised crime in Europe*. Dordrecht, Springer

Kleemans, E.R., M.E.I. Brienen & H.G. van de Bunt 2002. *Georganiseerde criminaliteit in Nederland : Tweede rapportage op basis van de WODC-monitor*. Meppel, Boom Juridische Uitgevers

Lampe, K. von 2001. "Not a Process of Enlightenment : The Conceptual History of Organized Crime in Germany and the United States of America". *Forum on Crime and Society* 2. 99–116

Lampe, K. von 2004a. "Making the second step before the first : Assessing organized crime: The case of Germany". *Crime, Law & Social Change* 42. 227–259

Lampe, K. von 2004b. "Measuring Organised Crime : A Critique of Current Approaches". Duyne, P.C. van, M. Jager, K. von Lampe & J.L. Newell eds.: *Threats and Phantoms of Organised Crime Corruption and Terrorism.* Nijmegen, Wolf Legal Publishers

Lampe, K. von 2007. "Criminals are not alone : Some observations on the social microcosm of illegal entrepreneurs". Duyne, P.C. van, A. Maljevic, M. van Dijck, K. von Lampe & J. Harvey eds.: *Crime Business and Crime Money in Europe : The Dirty Linen of Illicit Enterprise.* Nijmegen, Wolf Legal Publishers

Massari, M. and Mozini, P. 2004. "Dirty business in Italy : a case study of illegal trafficking in hazardous waste". *Global Crime* 3–4. 285–304

Morselli, C. 2005. *Contacts, Opportunities, and Criminal Enterprise.* Toronto, University of Toronto Press

Morselli, C., C. Giguere & K. Petit 2007. "The efficiency/security trade-off in criminal networks". *Social Networks* 29, 1. 143–153

Naylor, R.T. 2004. *Wages of crime : Black markets, illegal finance and the underworld economy.* Ithaca, Cornell University

Reuter, P. 1983. *Disorganised crime.* Cambridge, Massachusetts, MIT-press

Vander Beken, T. ed. 2005. *Organised crime and vulnerability of economic sectors : The European transports and music sector.* Antwerpen, Maklu

Vander Beken, T., K. Verpoest, A. Bucquoye and M. Defruytier 2005. "The vulnerability of economic sectors : the case of European road freight transport sector". Duyne, P.C. van, K. von Lampe, M. van Dyck & J.L. Newell eds.: *The organised crime economy : Managing crime markets in Europe.* Nijmegen, Wolf Legal Publishers

Vander Beken, T. ed. 2003. *Measuring organised crime in Europe : A feasibility study of a risk-based methodology across the European Union.* Antwerpen, Maklu

Vander Beken, T. 2004. "Risky business : a risk based methodology to measure organised crime". *Crime, Law and Social Change 5.* 471–516

Vettori, B. 2006. "Comparing data sources on organised crime across the EU : A first step towards an EU statistical apparatus". Duyne, P.C. van, A. Maljevic, M. van Dijck, K. von Lampe & J.L. Newell. *The organisation of crime for profit : Conduct, law and measurement.* Nijmegen, Wolf Legal Publishers http://www.assessingorganisedcrime.net deliverable 7

The study of organised crime: An assessment of the State of affairs

Klaus von Lampe

This article is concerned with the study of organised crime as a distinct field of research. What does it mean to "study organised crime"? For some, this question is an easy one to answer as it appears to imply the obvious: the study of "organised crime" is about studying organised crime. For others, the answer may be equally straightforward, but in the opposite direction: studying organised crime is about chasing ghosts, because there is no such thing as "organised crime" in the sense of a coherent phenomenon. For the majority however, the question is a difficult one, although not impossible to answer, this is because the answer is linked to the tricky and controversial question of definition: what is "organised crime"? Indeed, at first glance it seems logical to say that studying organised crime first of all requires clarity concerning the object of study (see e.g. Finckenauer 2005). However, I would argue that this is not true for a subject such as "organised crime" which is first and foremost a construct, a "notion vulgaire" in the Durkheimian sense (Durkheim 1973, 22–23), reflecting social reality as much as the emotions, prejudices and ideologies of those involved in the construction process. From a sociological perspective, such constructs cannot be accepted at face value. Rather, it is the duty of the social scientist to define and categorise the underlying phenomena and, through empirical observation, to explore the intricate links that exist that would justify placing all these diverse phenomena in one theoretical context. Accordingly, research on organised crime, at least in my understanding, does not have the notion of a coherent object of study as its starting point. On the contrary, the very purpose of the study of organised crime is to determine whether or not such a coherent phenomenon indeed exists. A definition of "organised crime", therefore, is a possible outcome rather than a precondition for the study of organised crime (Kelly 1986).

What needs to be done first is to try to bring the multifaceted imagery associated with the term "organised crime" into a preliminary form of order: What are people referring to when they talk about organised crime? Which persons, what events, which situations, places and so forth?

The second step is to examine the corresponding empirical manifestations to separate myth from reality and to develop an understanding of the dynamics and mechanisms at play.

At the end of a long research process, we may be able to determine the aspects of the social universe which can meaningfully be subsumed under this one concept of "organised crime", and which aspects call for different concepts.

In order for such a research program to unfold, researchers have to establish some common grounds on a terminological and conceptual level. However, little has been accomplished in this direction. Where "organised crime" is not just used as a noncommittal label, a certain degree of coordination and reciprocity of research has only been achieved by either taking mafia imagery as a common point of reference or by narrowing the focus to particular aspects. These aspects are then examined within fairly rigid conceptual frameworks, such as illegal markets or networks of co-offenders.

Despite the lack of a common understanding of its object of study, the study of organised crime has emerged as a field of research in its own right over the past 30 to 40 years. While American scholars dominated the scene in the 1960s and through the 1980s, Europe can stake a claim in recently becoming the centre of organised crime research. Based on a systematic, although certainly not exhaustive review of the academic literature, I am attempting here to identify some key trends regarding the institutionalisation of organised crime research as well as key research topics and methodology. While I have tried to include literature from Latin America, Africa, Asia and Australia, the focus is primarily on the situation in North America and Europe.[1]

The study of organised crime as an academic discipline

An academic discipline is constituted through a self-referential system comprising elements such as specialised journals, professional associations, university courses, and text-books. By this measure, the study of organised crime has emerged as at least a separate

---

[1] For a version of this paper focussing exclusively on the situation in Europe, and with a special emphasis on the funding of organised crime research, see K. von Lampe, Organised crime research in Europe: development and stagnation, in: P.C. van Duyne et al. (eds.), *European crime-markets at cross-roads: Extended and extending criminal Europe*, Nijmegen: Wolf Legal Publishers, forthcoming.

sub-discipline within the broad field of criminology and the social sciences. There are three journals with an exclusive or major focus on organised crime: *Trends in Organized Crime*, the journal which is affiliated with the International Association for the Study of Organized Crime (IASOC); *Crime, Law and Social Change*, which has the longest tradition and highest prestige among the three journals; and *Global Crime* which was previously published under the name *Transnational Organized Crime*. The editorial boards of these journals have partially overlapping membership, indicating the density of the overall network of scholars interested in organised crime. Two professional associations provide additional structure to the field: IASOC and the Standing Group Organized Crime of the European Consortium for Political Research (ECPR). The *eNewsletter Organized Crime* issued by the Standing Group is also an important publication platform aside from the three journals. Finally, there are regular meeting places for organised crime scholars, either at larger conferences such as those of the American and European societies of criminology, or at thematically focused conferences and workshops such as the Cross-border Crime Colloquia held annually at changing locations throughout Central and Eastern Europe.[2]

Courses on organised crime have been regularly taught in criminology and criminal justice programs in the United States for decades, with universities in other parts of the world, especially Europe, now following suit. A number of textbooks are available, of which the ones by Howard Abadinsky (Abadinsky 2007) and Jay Albanese (Albanese 2007) have the longest tradition, with first

---

[2] See the conference volumes produced as a result of the Cross-border Crime Colloquia under the co-editorship of Petrus C. van Duyne et al.

editions dating back to the 1980s. However, the first organised crime texts appeared as early as the mid-1970s, most notably Frederic Homer's underrated "Guns and Garlic" (Homer 1974; see also Pace & Style 1975). The recent publication of European textbooks, or textbook-like introductory volumes, on organised crime is an indicator of the increased importance of organised crime as a subject in European criminology curricula (Ignjatovic 1998; Johansen 1996; Wright 2006).

While scholars interested in organised crime are scattered all across the globe, certain centres of research activity have been established. Some of these research centres are institutionally independent, such as the Center for the Study of Democracy (CSD) in Sofia, Bulgaria; and the Institute for Security Studies (ISS) with the "Organised Crime & Money Laundering programme" of its Cape Town office in South Africa. Others are integrated into government structures, such as WODC in the Netherlands, the Council for Crime Prevention (Brå) in Sweden and the Institute of Criminology and Social Prevention (IKSP) in the Czech Republic. Some centres are affiliated with universities, such as the Centre for Information and Research on Organised Crime (CIROC) in the Netherlands; Transcrime in Italy; Ghent University's Institute for International Research on Criminal Policy (IRCP); the Terrorism, Transnational Crime and Corruption Center (TraCCC) at George Mason University in Virginia[3] with a branch office in Tbilisi (the capital of the former Soviet republic of Georgia); and the Nathanson Centre on Transnational Human Rights, Crime and Security (formerly: Nathanson Centre for the Study of Organized

---

[3] TraCCC moved from American University, Washington D.C., to George Mason University in 2007.

Crime and Corruption) at York University, Toronto. (Despite the recently expanded thematic focus, the latter has declared the intention of maintaining an interest in the study of organised crime.)

Some universities have become centres of organised crime research, not by virtue of formal structures but because of continuous research by scholars, including PhD-students, who have specialised in organised crime studies. In North America, these include, to cite a few examples, the University of Montreal, Canada; Rutgers University in Newark, New Jersey; San Diego State University, California; and John Jay College of Criminal Justice in New York. In Europe, Cardiff University in Wales; Tilburg University in the Netherlands and the University of Leuven in Belgium are among the academic institutions with a strong profile in organised crime research. Finally, several supranational research and documentation centres, which include the European Monitoring Centre for Drugs and Drug Addiction (EMCDDA) in Lisbon; the United Nations Office on Drugs and Crime in Vienna; and the Geneva-based International Organization for Migration (IOM), have made significant contributions to the study of organised crime in specific areas: drug trafficking, human trafficking and human smuggling to name but a few.

The three grand themes of the study of organised crime

There are three grand themes addressed in the academic literature under the broad heading of "organised crime": the meta level of the discourse on organised crime, the level of empirical manifestations of organised crime, and the level of counter measures.

Meta level: Construction of "organised crime" as a social problem

Quite a lot has been written about the construction of "organised crime" as a social problem.

The concept of "organised crime", this much seems clear, is an American invention, which has been exported to other parts of the world via the dual channels of Hollywood films and international law enforcement co-operation. The imported concept has then been superimposed onto heterogeneous crime landscapes and gone through various modifications and reinterpretations across time and space.

A number of authors have examined how the concepts of "organised crime" and "transnational organised crime" gained prominence first in the United States and later throughout the world (see e.g. Albanese 1988; Edwards & Gill 2002; Kelly 1978; von Lampe 1999; 2001; Luczak 2004; Massari 2003; Moore 1974; Smith 1975; 1991; Woodiwiss 1990; 2003). Two recurring themes can be found in this literature. There is, on the one hand, the issue of myth and reality and the apparent discrepancy between the certainty with which the concept is used in public discourse and the weak underlying knowledge base. On the other hand, there is the political dimension, the instrumentalization of the image of the threat of "organised crime" in order to legitimise new law enforcement measures and the associated infringement of civil liberties. It has been argued that the concept of "organised crime" was uncritically adopted outside the United States,[4] that it serves political and institutional interests and reproduces historical threat

---

[4] It should be noted that similar problems had already arisen within the United States owing to the contrast between the situation in the New York area and those parts of the country without a presence of Cosa Nostra families (see von Lampe, 2001: 107).

imagery rather than contributing to a better understanding of the social reality of crime. While this argumentation has some merits, one cannot ignore the fact that research in this area is fragmented and, with very few exceptions, no methodologically rigid and systematic studies on the process of constructing "organised crime" as a social problem have been conducted. Most of the literature is essayistic rather than analytical. It draws on small sets of sources, centred on particular events such as highly publicised parliamentary inquiries, and there is a tendency towards hedging conspiracy theories when it comes to explaining the political career of the concept of "organised crime". A widespread, at least implicit, allegation is that the concept of "organised crime" is a purposeful fabrication by law enforcement lobbyists who have sought to justify the expansion of police powers. However, in order to reach such a conclusion with any level of confidence, one must look behind the scenes, which would include the analysis of internal documents and interviews with key actors. Indeed, in all likelihood, such research would probably unearth more complex and complicated mechanisms in the construction of "organised crime" than are suggested by what can be termed the "law enforcement conspiracy theory". Accordingly, it seems safe to say that future researchers will encounter sufficient opportunities to significantly broaden, deepen, and revise current wisdom.

Empirical manifestations of organised crime

There is a slowly but steadily growing body of empirical literature on organised crime world-wide. Yet, it seems that the majority of contemporary work in the field has originated in Europe, with the Netherlands the most productive country. In order to obtain a better understanding of the course the study of organised crime is taking, it is helpful to sort the literature by central research topics or basic dimensions. In fact, when describing the object of the study of organised crime, one should address a number of different empirical phenomena that are examined in a rather loose conceptual context. These phenomena include "organised criminals" as a distinct category of offenders; the activities they are involved in; the associational patterns through which they are connected; and the power structures that subordinate these individuals and collectives to common or particular interests. Additionally, one must consider the relations between these individuals: structures and activities on the one hand, and the legal spheres of society on the other. These main facets of the indistinct overall picture are not equally addressed in the literature (see von Lampe 2006b; von Lampe et al. 2006).

Individual Offenders

Individual "organised" offenders are very rarely the focus of attention. This is in stark contrast to other fields of criminology, including the study of terrorism, where medical and psychological approaches enjoy some popularity. It is also in notable contrast to the gangster and mafioso stereotypes which dominate the public image of "organised crime". Other than Italian literature on the psyche of mafiosi (see ref. in Di Maria & Lo Verso 2007), Frank Bovenkerk's examination of the personality of mafia bosses, drawing on gangster biographies (Bovenkerk 2000), appears to be the only work specifically concerned with the psychological aspect of organised crime. A biographical approach is also adopted by Claudio Besozzi in his more general analysis of illicit entrepreneurs (Besozzi 2001). In a methodologically rigid study, Morselli and Tremblay (Morselli & Tremblay 2004) examined the relationship between levels of self-control (measured using Grasmick, Tittle, Bursik and Arneklev's twenty three item self-control scale) and the structure of criminal networks. They questioned 156 prison inmates, previously involved in money-oriented crimes, about their core (egocentric) criminal networks and found that, for illegal activities requiring ongoing social organisation, low self-control has a disruptive impact on criminal earnings by diminishing the abilities of offenders to fully exploit the opportunities rooted in their non-redundant criminal networks.

Others have addressed psychological aspects in broader discussions of illegal markets and criminal collectives (Canter & Alison 2000; van Duyne 2000). In the future, the emphasis on associational structures can be expected to become less prominent and the study of organised crime is predicted to move closer to mainstream criminology by incorporating the human factor in the analysis of criminal structures (von Lampe 2006b). This assumption is based on the concept that approaches aiming at explaining "organised crime" by the structure of criminal organisations, such as networks or organisations in the narrow sense of the word, tend to underestimate the importance of individual skills and characteristics in the creation and shaping of associational structures, and collective activities for that matter. To paraphrase a popular motto (Coles 2001), it may not be who you *are* but who you *know* that counts in "organised crime", although who you know may depend upon who you are and what social skills you have to a considerable extent.

Two other aspects that define stereotypes of "organised criminals" without being purely individualistic traits, have received some attention in the academic literature on organised crime: ethnicity and gender.

In public perception and in law enforcement statistics, organised crime tends to be associated with members of particular ethnic groups, although the specific links may vary across types of crime, illegal market level, geographical region and time. From the evidence available it seems that, in many instances, ethnic homogeneity among offenders (where it does exist) is not linked to ethnicity. Rather, it seems to be a reflection of underlying factors such as family ties or differential opportunity structures linked to geography; or the prevalence of certain ethnic groups may be a result of xenophobic discrimination (Bovenkerk 1998; O'Kane 1992; Paoli & Reuter 2008).

Gender has been discussed in the context of organised crime primarily in two ways, first with respect to the apparent predominance of men within criminal networks, and second with respect to the victimisation of women through organised criminal activity, namely human trafficking for sexual exploitation. In recent years, there has been a tendency to question formerly held views, which are to an extent parallel to perceived empirical changes in the relation between men and women, notably in the realm of traditional mafia associations (see e.g. Allum 2007; Siebert 2007). It is argued that, contrary to imagery of male domination, there is a significant incidence of women who occupy leading roles in criminal networks, including areas of crime where female victimisation is a characteristic (Calder 1995; Denton & O'Malley 1999; Graziosi 2001; Kleemans & Van de Bunt 1999; O'Kane 1992; Surtees 2008).

In the realms of both ethnicity and gender, it seems that there is considerable scope for future research. One such manifestation involves combining the findings of empirical studies on crime with insights from related disciplines, such as anthropology and gender studies.

Criminal Activities

"Organised crime" is associated with a wide range of criminal activities. Accordingly, specific types of crime or illegal markets may provide the frame of reference for scientific exploration, rather than studies focusing on "criminal groups" or geographical areas. This holds particularly true when "traditional organised crime" is not an issue, as is the case in the majority of countries other than the U.S., Italy, China and Japan,

Drug trafficking has traditionally received the greatest amount of attention in research on organised crime (see e.g. Van de Bunt, Kunst & Siegel 2002; Desroches 2005; Dorn, Otte & White 1999; Gruppo Abele 2003; Gruter & van de Mheen 2005; Pearson & Hobbs 2001; Zaitch 2002). Recently, however, the black market in cigarettes has emerged as a favourite object of study (Antonopoulos 2006; 2007; Beare 2003; Coker 2003; Dantinne 2001; van Dijck 2007; van Duyne 2003b; Hornsby & Hobbs 2007; Hozic 2004; Janssens et al. 2008; von Lampe 2002; 2003b; 2005b; 2006a; 2007; Markina 2007). Examples of other areas of crime explored by empirical research include human trafficking (Antonopoulos & Winterdyk 2005; Obradovic 2004; Spencer et al. 2006), illegal gambling (Liddick 1998; Reuter 1983), trafficking in stolen motor vehicles (Gerber & Killias 2003; Tremblay et al. 2001; Sieber & Bögel 1993), alcohol smuggling (Johansen 2005), illegal waste disposal (Gruppo Abele et al. 2003; Massari & Monzini 2004), maritime piracy (Eklöf 2005; Warren 2003), credit card fraud (Levi 2003), fencing (Sund et al. 2006; Weschke & Heine-Heiß 1990), black labour (van Duyne & Houtzager 2005; Carlström & Hedström 2007), and money laundering (van Duyne 2003a; Passas 1999; Suendorf 2001).

Patterns of Criminal Association

The question "How organised is organised crime?" appears to guide most researchers in the field, whether explicitly or implicitly. Donald Cressey's (Cressey 1969) interpretation of the American Mafia as synonymous with organised crime and similar in structure to a government and a large corporation (see e.g. Albini 1971; Smith 1975; Anderson 1979; Reuter 1983; Potter 1994), and the ensuing dispute has not been exclusively confined to the research community in the United States. Distancing from Cressey's "bureaucratic model" is a central component in the overall line of reasoning of quite a number of non-American authors also. Indeed, something of a consensus has developed which holds that the predominant structural pattern of criminal cooperation is characterised by webs of personal relations that are flexibly used by offenders to commit crimes. According to many empirical studies, cooperation typically occurs either on a contractual basis, that is in the form of supplier-consumer or ephemeral employer-employee relations, or on a partnership basis – in pairs or small groups with little overall horizontal or vertical integration (Adler 1985; Bruinsma & Bernasco 2004; Desroches 2005; Van Duyne 2003b; Johansen 2005; Junninen 2006; Gruppo Abele 2003; Kleemans & Van de Bunt 1999; von Lampe 2003b; Paoli 2003a; Pearson & Hobbs 2001; Reuter & Haaga 1989; Ruggiero & Khan 2007; Zaitch 2002).

Two challenges emerge in this situation. The first of which is to develop a sufficiently concise terminology in order to adequately capture the variation and fluidity of patterns of criminal association. The paucity of concepts, which is mirrored in the frequent use of ambiguous phrases like "loosely structured" or "network like" translates into a lack of analytical clarity. The second challenge lies in the application of network analytical tools. What would seem to be an obvious choice in instances where there is no form of structural integration of offenders, that is, to examine offender relations in terms of networks, has considerable limitations, of which the problem of missing and incomplete data may be the most difficult one to resolve. Missing data influence network analysis more than traditional statistical analyses (Chattoe & Hamill 2005; Knoke & Kuklinski 1982; Robins, Koskinen and Pattison 2008). At the same time, data are particularly likely to be missing in the case of criminal networks where researchers seldom have prior knowledge about all the relevant individuals. Furthermore, even if all individuals are known, researchers may then be unable to obtain the requisite information on all of them (Sparrow 1991). Proceeding with the analysis "in terms of what is known" (McAndrew 2000: 62) may make sense for some network measures, but not for all (Robins, Koskinen and Pattison 2008).

Criminal network analysis is also limited by the lack of depth of the available information. Often, data do not consistently go beyond merely stating that some form of contact exists between a given pair of actors. This level of information is only sufficient for certain research questions, such as the one addressed by a Swedish study which, based on co-offending data, explored the reach of criminal contacts of a set of drug traffickers. The study revealed that the 127 individuals convicted in connection with serious drug offences in Stockholm county, in 2003, had been in contact (either directly or indirectly) with at least 7,000 other individuals suspected of criminal involvement (Korsell et al. 2005). The authors took this to be evidence for the existence of a widespread criminal milieu. In other studies, network analysis has proven valuable in sorting through data sets involving large numbers of actors, especially in the initial phase of data analysis (see e.g. Finckenauer & Waring 1998; Giannakopoulos 2001; Natarajan 2000; 2006). Network analysis is also useful for addressing specific research questions such as criminal risk management (Morselli, Giguère & Petit 2007) and the relevance of actors from legitimate spheres for criminal operations (Morselli & Giguere 2006). Otherwise, the greatest value of the network concept seems to be that it forces researchers to adopt a bottom-up approach in the description and analysis of offender structures that is independent of popular imagery and constructs (Klerks 2003; von Lampe 2003a). Henner Hess' classical study of the Sicilian Mafia (Hess 1970), in which he breaks down the world of Cosa Nostra into different types of dyadic ties, is a good example of such a down-to-earth research strategy. However, there is a danger of falling to the other extreme by failing to acknowledge durable, vertically and horizontally differentiated offender structures when they are indeed present. To avoid this pitfall, the examination of vertical integration and differentiation need to be incorporated in criminal network analysis (Natarajan 2000).

Overarching Power Structures

Above the micro-level of entrepreneurial offenders and offender collectives, overarching structures can be found which claim control over a given territory, such as a town or region, or an illegal market or illegal-market level, furthering particular or common interests. Alan Block has coined the term "power syndicate", as opposed to "enterprise syndicate", to denote this kind of criminal structure (Block 1983: 13). Phenomena falling into this category have mostly been identified and studied in Southern Italy (Gambetta 1993; Hess 1970; Paoli 2003b), Russia (Varese 2001), Japan (Hill 2003) and the United States (Anderson 1979; Haller 1991; Reuter 1983). An interesting question that has been raised recently pertains to the extent to which these territorially based groups have the capacity to migrate and reproduce their position of power, this may also extend to the legal economy, in areas or even countries outside their traditional sphere of influence (Varese 2004; 2006).

Illegal-Legal Nexus

The individuals, structures, and activities associated with "organised crime" do not exist in a social vacuum. Instead, they are connected with their surroundings in various ways.

One aspect is the "social embeddedness of organized crime" (Kleemans & van de Bunt 1999) in certain social strata, milieux, or ethnic communities. Anomie theory has proved an obvious choice in order to explain this connection with regard to migrant communities (Bovenkerk 1998), whereas concepts and theories derived from social and cultural anthropology have been applied to indigenous "organised crime" phenomena such as the Sicilian Mafia (Cottino 1999; Hessinger 2002). However, not all "organised crime" is necessarily (sub-)culturally rooted. Research on cigarette smuggling and on a wide range of other areas of crime in different countries suggests that, to a considerable extent, offenders involved in illegal market activities do not have a wider criminal background and apparently start their criminal careers fairly late in life (Desroches 2005; van Dijck 2007; van Duyne 2003b; Janssens et al. 2008; Kleemans & van de Poot 2008; von Lampe 2005b).

Many discussions about the links between the illegal and legal spheres of society are framed in the concept of corruption. An associated image depicts "organised criminals" neutralizing law enforcement by bribing and intimidating police officials, prosecutors and judges. Another image is that of "organised criminals" in alliance with political and business elites. Relatively little empirical research has been conducted in these areas and the bulk of the literature refers to conditions in the United States, Southern Italy and Eastern Europe; few studies specifically address the dimension of "organised crime" (see e.g. Center for the Study of Democracy 2004; Galli 1994; Gardiner 1970; Maljevic et al. 2006; Newell 2006; Paoli 2003b; Potter 1994; Potter & Gaines 1995; Varese 2001).

Similar to the infiltration of government there is a concern about the infiltration of the legal economy by "organised crime". This may take the form of legal businesses falling under the control of criminal groups, legal businesses and criminals establishing collusive links, or the formation of criminal networks within the legal business sector (Albanese 1995; Dorn et al. 2007; Paoli 1995; Ruggiero 2000). Finally, in an extension of the regulation of illegal markets, criminal groups may provide quasi-governmental functions such as debt collection, conflict resolution and protection from competition for legal businesses (Gambetta 1993; Reuter 1985; Varese 2001; Volkov 2000).

Dutch criminologist Jan van Dijk recently assumed an interesting approach to the study of "power syndicates" and criminal influence on legal business. He combined various types of data to create what he terms a "Composite Organized Crime Index (COCI)" (van Dijk 2007: 42). A central component of this index is a survey by the World Economic Forum (WEF) delivered to business executives in over one hundred countries. One item in the questionnaire reads as follows:

> Organized crime (e.g. mafia-oriented racketeering, extortion) in your country (1=imposes significant

costs on businesses, 7=does not impose significant costs on business).
(World Economic Forum, 2005, 565)

Van Dijk put the average rankings of countries on the WEF surveys of 1997 to 2003 alongside assessments by a consultancy firm, the Merchant International Group, of the prevalence of different types of organised crime (drugs, arms, people trafficking), and national rates of unsolved murders. Van Dijk found that all of these measures varied fairly consistently cross-nationally. By this measure, Oceania and Western and central Europe had the lowest scores of 33 and 35, respectively, indicating low levels of "organised crime", while Eastern Europe, Central Asia and Transcaucasia, and the Caribbean ranked the highest with a score of 70 (van Dijk 2007: 42). The values are not further broken down in van Dijk's paper, although it is interesting to note that, from the WEF data alone, using the 2005 survey figures, the situation is more heterogeneous. That is to say that "organised crime" in the Netherlands appears to have a strong influence on legal business in the perception of the management elite; a stronger one than in countries like Estonia, Uruguay, or Ghana (World Economic Forum 2005: 565). Future research will reveal how robust the insights gained from survey data are, but the combination of various data sources appears to be well worth further exploration.

Organised crime in the context of a geographical area

An approach that touches on most, if not all, of these aspects within one overall framework is the examination of "organised crime" in the context of a particular geographical area. Studies range from neighbourhoods (Standing 2006), towns (Chambliss 1978; Potter

1994), and counties (Potter & Gaines 1995) to entire countries (Galeotti 1998). However, it seems that, the broader the area under study, the more difficult it is to produce a comprehensive analysis with sufficient detail due to the complexities that have to be taken into account.

Organised crime in history

The difficulties in attaining a comprehensive picture increase when historical events and conditions are examined. A number of historical studies of organised crime have been produced in recent years, focusing on the situation in particular places (Block 1983; Dickson-Gilmore & Woodiwiss 2008; Egmond 1993; McIllwain 2004), on particular crimes (Eklöf 2005; Johansen 1994), or on particular criminal groupings (Catanzaro 1992; Hartmann & von Lampe 2008; Lupo 2002; McIllwain 2001). As Jeff McIllwain, perhaps the most outspoken advocate of an historical approach to the study of organised crime, has argued, history adds perspective, it shows that what is perceived as new may not be so new after all, it may also serve to retrospectively test hypotheses (McIllwain 2004: 189). On the other hand, organised crime research is notoriously characterised by difficulties in accessing data. The passing of time aggravates, rather than minimises these difficulties; at least when the period under investigation is so far back that no witnesses are left to tell their story. This inevitably limits the number of suitable objects of historical study.

Countermeasures

The third major thematic area defining the study of organised crime, apart from the meta-level of the construction of "organised crime" and the empirical level of "organised crime" phenomena, concerns countermeasures adopted against "organised crime". Generally, countermeasures have been adopted in the form of modified and newly introduced material and procedural criminal law (Goredema 2001; Goredema & Botha 2004; Paoli & Fijnaut 2006),[5] in part driven by international agreements and conventions (Albrecht & Fijnaut 2002; McClean 2007), institutional changes in law enforcement and the criminal justice system (Pütter 1998; Segell 2007), and administrative law (Huisman & Nelen 2007; Köbben 2002). These measures, and especially their legal ramifications, have been described in great detail. However, relatively little research has been conducted on their implementation and efficacy with regard to reducing and preventing "organised crime" (Maltz 1990). The major weakness appears to be the lack of a clear understanding of the nature, extent, and developmental trends of "organised crime" as a valid measuring stick. In the majority of cases, the literature relies on prima facie plausibility, and on politically and media induced imagery regarding the reality of "organised crime"; alternatively it applies criteria that have nothing to do with the crime situation as such, but with bureaucratic effectiveness or civil rights issues (see e.g. Kinzig 2004; Vettori 2006a).

Some efforts have been made by scholars to tackle the deficiencies in the existing knowledgebase on "organised crime", which are becoming apparent not only in the evaluation of countermeasures, but more generally in the areas of criminal policy and intelligence-led policing. One such undertaking has been to make better use of existing statistical data, especially in a cross-national perspective, on particular areas of crime, such as human trafficking (Di Nicola &

---

[5] An interesting collection of national overviews of anti-organised crime measures is contained in the volume "Organized Crime in Europe", edited by C. Fijnaut and L. Paoli (Dordrecht: Springer, 2004).

Cauduro 2007), or on organised crime in general (Vettori 2006b). Another undertaking aims at utilizing a broader range of data for the purpose of proactive assessments of "organised crime" in the form of risk analysis, scenario building and model construction (Black et al. 2000; Vander Beken & Defruytier 2004; Vander Beken et al. 2004; Verfaillie & Vander Beken 2008; Williams & Godson 2002).

An alternative direction has been proposed by the EU-funded "Assessing Organised Crime" project. Without developing a comprehensive conceptual and theoretical framework, the project has outlined a mechanism, the New European Common Approach (NECA); this advocates not only more effective use of existing law enforcement data for strategic crime analysis, but also the future integration of strategic crime analysis and scientific research. The idea behind NECA is that the existence of a sufficient knowledge base for valid and meaningful assessments of "organised crime" cannot simply be pretended. Instead, it needs to be systematically built bottom-up in both the medium and long run (Assessing Organised Crime Research Consortium 2007; van Duyne 2007; von Lampe 2005c).

Empirical research and theory building

The study of "organised crime" is not fundamentally different from any other area of social science research in that it is confronted by problems in finding good data, and meaningfully describing, systematizing and explaining the social phenomena that have been observed.

Collecting data on "organised crime"

All means of data collection common in sociological research can, and have been, utilised in the study of "organised crime": observations, interviews and text analysis. Participant observations have been rare and not always without risk. Two of the earliest Mafia studies, Anton Blok's exploration of the Mafia in a Sicilian Village (Blok 1974) and Francis Ianni's exploration of the social life of a New York Mafia family (Ianni & Reuss-Ianni 1972), fall within this category; as does Patty Adler's similarly classic study of upper level drug dealers in California (Adler 1985). An example where the risks of participant observations have materialized is provided by a yet unpublished PhD-project in Poland, which has become the subject of a book by the German investigative journalist, Jürgen Roth (Roth 2005). Aneta M. took a job in a bar that served as a meeting place for the Polish underworld with the purpose of writing a doctoral thesis on organised crime. Roth alleges that owing of pressure exerted by criminal circles, Aneta M. was unable to obtain her doctoral degree from the University of Szczecin, Poland, where she had been based while conducting her research. A daring approach was also adopted in a study of smuggling and corruption in Georgia, where researchers posed as smugglers for the purpose of participant observation and covert interviewing (Kukhianidze, Kupatadze & Gotsiridze 2004).

In the American research tradition, direct interaction with offenders as a method of data collection has always played an important role alongside interviews with law enforcement officials and other experts (see e.g. Thrasher 1927; Albini 1971; Potter 1994). In Europe, for a long time, interview-based studies in the area of organised crime meant studies drawing primarily or exclusively on expert accounts, in most cases that of police investigators (Kerner

1973; Mack & Kerner 1975; Rebscher & Vahlenkamp 1988; Sieber & Bögel 1993). In recent years, however, a general trend towards offender interviews either as a prominent source amongst others (see e.g. Johansen 2004; Ruggiero & South 1995), or as the primary data source has emerged, at least in North America and Europe. A few studies, especially those with the largest sample sizes, involve incarcerated offenders or individuals, namely informants, otherwise under the control of the criminal justice system (see e.g. Decker & Townsend Chapman 2008; Desroches 2005; Dorn, Oette & White 1998; Kinzig 2004; Matrix Knowledge Group 2007; Pearson & Hobbs 2001; Reuter & Haaga 1989). Some studies have used both incarcerated and non-incarcerated offenders (see e.g. Junninen 2006; Ruggiero & Khan 2006; Zaitch 2002), while others exclusively rely on non-incarcerated offenders (see e.g. Antonopoulos 2006; Hobbs 2001; Hornsby & Hobbs 2007; see also the special issue "Interviewing 'Organized Criminals'" of the journal *Trends in Organized Crime*, 11(1), 2008). These latter studies contradict the commonly held notion that "organised criminals" are unapproachable for research purposes.

Text analysis is most frequently used in the study of organised crime in connection with official and media reports (see e.g. von Lampe 2006a), but it is also employed when criminal files and investigative files comprise the primary basis of data (see e.g. Anderson 1979; van Duyne 1996; 2003b; Herz 2005; Hess 1970; Kinzig 2004; von Lampe 2005b; 2007; Reuter 1983; Suendorf 2001). With the increasing computerization of police work, it can be expected that the study of organised crime will routinely involve the analysis of electronically stored data (see e.g. van Duyne 2003a; Korsell et al. 2005).

Systematization

No attempt is made here to comment in detail on the different ways researchers have been systematizing their areas of study.[6] What can be said, although with some caution, is that the most valuable categories and classifications have been proposed and elaborated by North-American authors, which may reflect the chronology of research efforts. Valuable classifications include the dichotomies of predatory and market-based crime (Naylor 2003), of "power syndicates" and "enterprise syndicates" (Block 1983), of economic and non-economic criminal structures (Haller 1992), and the distinction between purely market-based criminal relations, criminal networks ties, and transactional links within criminal organizations (enterprises) (Smith 1994).

Explanation

In a similar vein, it is beyond the scope of this paper to review the various theoretical propositions found in the organised crime literature in depth. Moreover, it seems that the most influential theoretical propositions, however fragmented they may be, originate in North America. When one thinks of global approaches to explaining "organised crime", one is immediately reminded of Robert K. Merton's anomie theory which is closely linked to the American experience of immigrant criminal groups (Merton 1957; see also Bell 1953; Cloward & Ohlin1960). More focused theoretical propositions aim at explaining the emergence (Felson 2006; Smith 1994) and the structure of illegal enterprises (Reuter 1983; Smith 1994; Southerland & Potter 1993). These theoretical

---

[6] For a more in-depth analysis of some of the international organised-crime literature, see von Lampe et. al. (2006).

approaches have been reflected in the international research literature fairly extensively. Some propositions, in particular those of Peter Reuter, have been confirmed, although predominantly on a rhetorical level rather than in the form of rigorous testing. This is particularly problematic because Reuter developed his hypotheses in investigations of crime phenomena – illegal gambling and loan sharking – in manifestations that seem to be quite specific to the situation in the United States and New York City in particular (Reuter 1983).

There is probably only one theoretical approach originating outside of North America that has assumed any general significance: Diego Gambetta's notion of mafia-like associations thriving as industries of protection in low-trust social environments (Gambetta 1993). In much the same way that this proposition has been tested in different social contexts (Hill 2003; Varese 2001), all the facets of the subject area of "organised crime" need to be explored in different historical and socio-geographical settings in order to be able to develop and test hypotheses and theories through comparison.

Concluding remarks

Within the limits of this article, I am only able to give a rough and inevitably sketchy outline of the state of organised crime research. From a global perspective, it appears that a shift in weight has taken place over the past 20 years, from North America to Europe. This shift is in terms of both the number and diversity of empirical research projects, and also in the reality of organised crime. Following the fall of the Iron Curtain myriad, new, although not necessarily novel, manifestations of criminal structures and illegal markets have emerged in ever-changing patterns. These have been the subject of numerous, mostly descriptive studies. However, the opportunities for comparative research and theory building have not yet been systematically exploited.

There are three fundamental challenges defining the future of organised crime research. The first one is to ensure continuity of research in order to go beyond merely reproducing, and responding to, the clichés that appear in the media and in political debates at irregular intervals. Continuity means, first of all, an ongoing research process which contributes to a cumulative body of knowledge. It also means that a network of researchers can develop to combine resources and connect different countries and different areas of specialization within the field of "organised crime" and different academic disciplines. Continuity of research also means that relations of trust can develop between researchers and law enforcement practitioners. This is particularly important because trust is often the precondition in order for data to become available for scientific analysis in this security-sensitive area of study.

Indeed, access to data is the second major challenge in the study of organised crime. While researchers have been both innovative and persistent in their efforts to obtain information from offenders, law enforcement sources, victims and experts, these successes cannot be taken for granted. Training of young researchers, further development of methodologies and an increasing receptivity to the needs of research on the part of law enforcement agencies and politics seem to be key for more and better organised crime research in the future.

The third major challenge is to maintain or win independence from outside influences. In many countries of the world, organised crime researchers find themselves in direct conflict with powerful interest groups in political and business spheres. Even in countries where criminal structures are apparently less pervasive and powerful, independent research is hampered or rendered impossible by biases towards particular topics. Accordingly research questions and outcomes are typically built into funding schemes and there is differential access to data that favours embedded, uncritical researchers (see e.g. Weitzer 2007: 460). Research taking place within these confines cannot be expected to yield meaningful results.

To the extent that an environment conducive to critical empirical research and theory building does exist, the onus to move ahead is on the community of organised crime researchers. As I have argued elsewhere (von Lampe 2002), research projects need to be designed in such a manner that they are reciprocally meaningful in order to be able to contribute to a cumulative body of knowledge about phenomena that are variously subsumed under the pre-scientific umbrella concept of organised crime. In order to attain such compatibility, two requirements must be met. Firstly, middle-range concepts well below the lofty level of "organised crime" need to be defined and agreed upon; secondly, the phenomena defined by these middle-range concepts need to be investigated: within one context and in as many social and historical settings as possible. In the end, the concept of "organised crime" may well evaporate; nevertheless, the study of "organised crime" would have proved itself to be an endeavor which addresses some substantial concerns, ones that cannot simply be argued away solely because they are articulated using an often abused buzzword.

References

Abadinsky, H. 2007. *Organized Crime*. 8th ed. Belmont, CA, Thomson Wadsworth

Adler, P. 1985. *Wheeling and Dealing : An Ethnography of an Upper-Level Drug Dealing and Smuggling Community*. New York, Columbia University Press

Albanese, J. 1988. "Government perceptions of organized crime : the presidential commissions 1967 and 1987". *Federal Probation* 52, 1. 58–63

Albanese, J.S. 1995. "Where organized and white collar crime meet : predicting the infiltration of legitimate business" Albanese, Jay ed.: *Contemporary Issues in Organized Crime*. Monsey, NY, Criminal Justice Press. 35–60

Albanese, J.S. 2007. *Organized Crime in our Times*. 5th ed. Newark, NJ, LexisNexis

Albini, J.L. 1971. *The American Mafia : Genesis of a Legend*, New York, Meredith Corporation

Albrecht, H.J. & C. Fijnaut eds. 2002. *The containment of transnational organized crime : Comments on the UN Convention of December 2000*. Freiburg, Max Planck Institute for Foreign and International Penal Law

Albrecht, P-A. 2002. *Kriminologie : Ein Studienbuch*. Munich, C.H. Beck

Allum, F. 2007. "Doing It for Themselves or Standing in for Their Men? Women in the Neapolitan Camorra (1950–2003)". Giovanni Fiandaca ed.: *Women and the Mafia : Female Roles in Organized Crime Structures*. New York, Springer. 9–17

Anderson, A.G. 1979. *The business of organized crime : a Cosa Nostra family*. Stanford, CA, Hoover Institution Press

Antonopoulos, G.A. 2006. "Cigarette smuggling : A case study of a smuggling network in Greece". *European Journal of Crime, Criminal Law and Criminal Justice* 14, 3. 239–255

Antonopoulos, G.A. 2007 "Cigarette Smugglers : A Note on Four 'Unusual Suspects'". *Global Crime* 8, 4. 393–398

Antonopoulos, G.A. & J. Winterdyk 2006. "The smuggling of migrants in Greece : An examination of its social organization". *European Journal of Criminology* 3, 4. 439–461

Assessing Organized Crime Research Consortium 2007. *Assessing Organized Crime by a New Common European Approach : Final Report.* Assessing Organized Crime project, Deliverable 33, 15 February

Beare, M.E. 2003. "Organized Corporate Criminality : Corporate Complicity in Tobacco Smuggling". Beare, Margaret E. ed.: *Critical Reflections on Transnational Organized Crime Money Laundering and Corruption.* Toronto, University of Toronto Press. 183–206

Bell, D. 1953. "Crime as an American Way of Life". *The Antioch Review* 13, 2. 131–145

Besozzi, C. 2001. *Wohin mit der Beute? Eine biographische Untersuchung zur Inszenierung illegalen Unternehmertums.* Berne, Haupt

Black, C., T.V. Beken, B. Frans & M. Paternotte 2000. *Reporting on Organized Crime : A Shift from Description to Explanation in the Belgian Annual Report on Organized Crime.* Antwerp, Maklu

Block, A. 1983. *East Side, West Side : Organizing Crime in New York 1930–1950.* New Brunswick, Transaction

Block, A. 1974. *The Mafia of a Sicilian Village 1860 – 1960 : a study of violent peasant entrepreneurs.* Oxford, Basil Blackwell

Bovenkerk, F. 1998. "Organized Crime and Ethnic Minorities : Is There a Link?". *Transnational Organized Crime* 4, 3&4. 109–126

Bovenkerk, F. 2000. "Wanted: 'Mafia boss' – Essay on the personology of organized crime". *Crime, Law and Social Change* 33, 3. 225–242

Bruinsma, G. & W. Bernasco 2004. "Criminal groups and transnational illegal markets : A more detailed examination on the basis of Social Network Theory", *Crime, Law and Social Change* 41, 1. 79–94

Bunt, H. van de, D. Kunst & D. Siegel 2003. *XTC over de grens : Een studie naar XTC-koeriers en kleine smokkelaars*. The Hague, Boom Juridische uitgevers

Bunt, H. van de & C. van der Schoot 2003. *Prevention of Organized Crime: A situational approach*. The Hague, WODC

Canter, D. & L. Alison eds. 2000. *The Social Psychology of Crime : Groups, Teams and Networks*. Aldershot, Ashgate

Carlström, A. & H.L. Hedström 2007. *Fina Fasader med Fixade Fakturor : Kriminella entreprenader i byggbranschen*. Stockholm, Brå

Catanzaro, R. 1992. *Men of respect : A social history of the Sicilian Mafia*. New York, The Free Press

Center for the Study of Democracy 2004. *Partners in Crime : The Risks of Symbiosis between the Security Sector and Organized Crime in Southeast Europe*. Sofia, Center for the Study of Democracy

Chambliss, W.J. 1978. *On the Take : From Petty Crooks to Presidents*. Bloomington, IN, Indiana University Press

Chattoe, E. & H. Hamill 2005. "It's Not Who You Know – It's What You Know About People You Don't Know That Counts : Extending the Analysis of Crime Groups as Social Networks", *British Journal of Criminology* 45, 6. 860–876

Cloward, R.A. & L. Ohlin 1960. *Delinquency and Opportunity : A Theory of Delinquent Gangs*. New York, The Free Press

Coker, D. 2003. "Smoking May not Only be Hazardous to Your Health but also to World Political Stability : The European Union's Fight Against Cigarette Smuggling Rings that Benefit Terrorism". *European Journal of Crime Criminal Law and Criminal Justice* 11, 4. 350–376

Coles, N. 2001. "It's not what you know – It's who you know that counts : Analysing serious crime groups as social networks". *The British Journal of Criminology* 41, 4. 580–594

Cottino, A. 1999. "Sicilian cultures of violence : The interconnections between organized crime and local society". *Crime, Law and Social Change* 32, 2. 103–113

Cressey, D.R. 1969. *Theft of the Nation : the structure and operations of organized crime in America*. New York, Harper & Row

Dantinne, M. 2001. "Contrebande de cigarettes: un exemple moderne de délinquance d'entreprise". *Revue Internationale de Criminologie et de Police Technique et Scientifique* 54, 1. 3–25

Decker, S. H. & M. Townsend Chapman 2008. *Drug Smugglers on Drug Smuggling : Lessons from the Inside*. Philadelphia, PA, Temple University Press

Denton, B. & P. O'Malley 1999. "Gender, Trust and Business : Women Drug Dealers in the Illicit Economy". *British Journal of Criminology* 39, 4. 513–530

Desroches, F. J. 2005. *The Crime That Pays : Drug Trafficking and Organized Crime in Canada*. Toronto, Canadian Scholars' Press

Dickson-Gilmore, J. & M. Woodiwiss 2008. "The history of native Americans and the misdirected study of organised crime". *Global Crime* 9, 1&2. 66–83

Dijck, M. van 2007. "Cigarette shuffle : organising tobacco tax evasion in the Netherlands". Duyne, P.C. van, A. Maljevic, M. van Dijck, K. von Lampe and J. Harvey eds.: *Crime business and crime money in Europe : The dirty linen of illicit enterprise*. Nijmegen, Wolf Legal Publishers

Dijk, J. van 2007. "Mafia markers : assessing organized crime and its impact upon societies". *Trends in Organized Crime* 10, 4. 39–56

Di Maria, F. & G. Lo Verso 2007. "Women in Mafia Organizations". Giovanni Fiandaca ed.: *Women and the Mafia : Female Roles in Organized Crime Structures*. New York, Springer. 87–101

Di Nicola, A. & A. Cauduro 2007. "Review of Official Statistics on Trafficking in Human Beings for Sexual Exploitation and their Validity in the 25 EU Member States from Official Statistics to Estimates of the Phenomenon". Savona, Ernesto U. & Sonia Stefanizzi eds.: *Measuring Human Trafficking : Complexities And Pitfalls*. New York, Springer. 73–94

Dorn, N., S. van Daele & T. Vander Beken 2007. "Reducing Vulnerabilities to Crime of the European Waste Management Industry : the Research Base and the Prospects for Policy". *European Journal of Crime, Criminal Law and Criminal Justice* 15, 1. 23–36

Dorn, N., M. Levi & L. King 2005. *Literature review on upper level drug trafficking*. London: Home Office, Home Office Online Report 22/05

Dorn, N., L. Oette & S. White 1999. "Drugs importation and the bifurcation of risk : capitalization cut outs and organized crime". *British Journal of Criminology* 38, 4. 537–560

Durkheim, É. 1973. *Les Règles de la Méthode Sociologique*. Paris, Presses Universitaires de France

Duyne, P.C. van 1996. "The phantom and threat of organized crime". *Crime, Law and Social Change* 24, 4. 341–377

Duyne, P.C. van 2000. "Mobsters are human too : Behavioral science and organized crime investigation". *Crime, Law and Social Change* 34, 4. 369–390

Duyne, P.C. van 2003a. "Money laundering policy : fears and facts". Duyne, P.C. van, K. von Lampe & J.L. Newell eds.: *Criminal Finances and Organising Crime in Europe*. Nijmegen, Wolf Legal Publishers. 67–104

Duyne, P.C. van 2003b. "Organizing cigarette smuggling and policy making ending up in smoke". *Crime, Law and Social Change* 39, 3. 285–317

Duyne, P.C. van 2004. "The creation of a threat image : Media, policy making and organized crime". Duyne, P.C. van, M. Jager, K. von Lampe & J.L. Newell eds.: *Threats and Phantoms of Organized Crime, Corruption and Terrorism : Critical European Perspectives*. Nijmegen, Wolf Legal Publishers. 21–50

Duyne, P.C. van 2007. "The New European Common Approach to Assessing Organized Crime (NECA)". *Standing Group Organized Crime eNewsletter* 6, 1

Duyne, P.C. & M.J. Houtzager 2005. "Criminal subcontracting in the Netherlands : The Dutch 'koppelbaas' as crime-entrepreneur". Duyne, P.C. van, K. von Lampe, M. van Dijck & J.L. Newell eds.; *The organized crime economy : Managing crime markets in Europe*. Nijmegen, Wolf Legal Publishers

Edwards, A. & P. Gill 2002. "The politics of transnational organized crime : discourse reflexivity and the narration of threat". *British Journal of Politics and International Relations* 4, 2. 245–270

Egmond, F. 1993. *Underworlds : organized crime in the Netherlands 1650–1800*. Cambridge, MA, Polity Press

Eklöf, S. 2005. *The Return of Piracy : Decolonization and International Relations in a Maritime Border Region (the Sulu Sea), 1959–63*. Lund, Lund University, Centre for East and South-East Asian Studies, Working Paper No. 15

European Monitoring Centre for Drugs and Drug Addiction (EMCDDA) 2006. *Annual Report 2006.* The State of the Drugs Problem in Europe. Lisbon, EMCDDA

Felson, M. 2006. *The Ecosystem for Organized Crime. HEUNI Paper 26.* Helsinki, HEUNI

Fijnaut, C., F. Bovenkerk, G. Bruinsma & H. van de Bunt 1998. *Organized crime in the Netherlands.* The Hague, Kluwer Law International

Finckenauer, J.O. 2005. "Problems of definition : What is organized crime?". *Trends in Organized Crime* 8, 3. 63–83

Finckenauer, J.O. & E.J. Waring 1998. *Russian Mafia in America : immigration culture and crime.* Boston, MA, Northeastern University Press

Galeotti, Mark 1998. "Turkish organized crime : where state crime and rebellion conspire". *Transnational Organized Crime* 4, 1. 25–41

Galli, G. 1994. *Staatsgeschäfte : Affären, Skandale, Verschwörungen- Das unterirrdische Italien 1943–1990.* Hamburg, Europäische Verlagsanstalt

Gambetta, D. 1993. *The Sicilian Mafia : The Business of Private Protection.* Cambridge, MA, Harvard University Press

Gardiner, J.A. 1970. *The Politics of Corruption : Organized Crime in an American City.* New York, Russell Sage Foundation

Gerber, J. & M. Killias 2003. "The Transnationalization of Historically Local Crime : Auto Theft in Western Europe and Russia Markets". *European Journal of Crime, Criminal Law and Criminal Justice* 11, 2. 215–226

Giannakopoulos, N. 2001. *Criminalité organisée et corruption en Suisse.* Berne, Haupt

Goredema, C. ed. 2001. *Organised Crime in Southern Africa : Assessing Legislation.* Pretoria, Institute for Security Studies

Goredema, C. & A. Botha 2004. "African Commitments to Combating Organised Crime and Terrorism : A Review of Eight NEPAD Countries". Nairobi, African Human Security Initiative

Graziosi, M. 2001. "Women, the Mafia and Legal Safeguards". *Forum on Crime and Society* 1, 2. 129–134

Gruppo, A. 2003. *Synthetic Drugs Trafficking in Three European Cities : Major Trends and the Involvement of Organized Crime.* Turin, Gruppo Abele

Gruppo, A & L. Nomos 2003. *The Illegal Trafficking in Hazardous Waste in Italy and Spain : Final Report.* Rome, GEPEC-EC

Gruter, P. & D. van de Mheen 2005. "Dutch cocaine trade : The perspective of Rotterdam cocaine retail dealers". *Crime, Law and Social Change* 44, 1. 19–33

Haller, Mark H. 1991. *Life Under Bruno : The Economics of an Organized Crime Family.* Conshohocken, PA, Pennsylvania Crime Commission

Haller, M. H. 1992. "Bureaucracy and the Mafia : An Alternative View". *Journal of Contemporary Criminal Justice* 8, 1. 1–10

Hartmann, A. & K. von Lampe 2008. "The German underworld and the *Ringvereine* from the 1890s through the 1950s". *Global Crime* 9, 1&2. 108–135

Herz, A.L. 2005. *Menschenhandel : Eine empirische Untersuchung zur Strafverfolgungspraxis.* Berlin, Duncker & Humblot

Hess, H. 1970. *Mafia : Zentrale Herrschaft und lokale Gegenmacht.* Tübingen, Mohr

Hessinger, P. 2002. "Mafia und Mafiakapitalismus als totales soziales Phänomen : Eine vergleichende Perspektive auf die Entwicklung in Italien und Russland". *Leviathan – Zeitschrift für Sozialwissenschaft* 30, 4. 482–508

Hill, P.B.E. 2003. *The Japanese Mafia : Yakuza, Law, and the State.* New York, Oxford University Press

Hobbs, D. 2001. "The Firm : Organizational Logic and Criminal Culture on a Shifting Terrain". *British Journal of Criminology* 41, 4. 549–560

Hobbs, D. 2004. "The Nature and Representation of Organized Crime in the United Kingdom". Fijnaut, Cyrille & Letizia Paoli eds.: *Organized Crime in Europe : Concepts, Patterns and Control Policies in the European Union and Beyond.* Dordrecht, Springer. 413–434

Homer, F. D. 1974. *Guns and Garlic : Myths and Realities of Organized Crime.* West Lafayette, IN, Purdue University Press

Hornsby, R. & D. Hobbs 2007. "A Zone of Ambiguity : The Political Economy of Cigarette Bootlegging". *British Journal of Criminology* 47, 4. 551–571

Hozic, A.A. 2004. "Between the Cracks : Balkan Cigarette Smuggling". *Problems of Post-Communism* 51, 3. 35–44

Huisman, W. & H. Nelen 2007. "Gotham unbound Dutch style : The administrative approach to organized crime in Amsterdam". *Crime, Law and Social Change* 48, 3–5. 87–103

Ianni, F.A.J. & E. Reuss-Ianni 1972. *A Family Business : Kinship and Social Control in Organized Crime.* New York, Russell Sage Foundation

Ignjatovi, Ð. 1998. *Organizovani Kriminalitet, drugi deo, Kriminoloshka analiza stanya u svetu.* Belgrade, Politsiska Akademiya

Janssens, J., T. Vander Beken, K. Verpoest, A. Balcaen & F. Vander Laenen 2008. "Crossing geographical, legal and moral boundaries : the Belgian cigarette black market". *Tobacco Control* 17,1. 60–65

Johansen, P.O. 1994. *Markedet som ikke ville dø : Forbudstiden og de illegale alkoholmarkedene i Norge og USA.* Oslo, Rusmiddeldirektoratet

Johansen, P.O. 1996. *Nettverk i gråsonen.* Oslo, Ad Notam

Johansen, P.O. 2004. *Den illegale Spriten : Fra forbutstid til polstreik*. Oslo, Unipub

Johansen, P.O. 2005. "Organized crime, Norwegian style". Duyne, P.C. van, K. von Lampe, M. van Dijck & J.L. Newell eds.: *The Organized Crime Economy : Managing Crime Markets in Europe*. Nijmegen, Wolf Legal Publishers

Junninen, M. 2006. *Adventurers and risk-takers : Finnish professional criminals and their organisations in the 1990s cross-border criminality*. Helsinki, HEUNI

Kelly, R.J. 1978. *Organized crime : a study in the production of knowledge by law enforcement specialists*. [Doctoral dissertation]. Ann Arbor, MI, University Microfilms International

Kelly, R.J. 1986. "Criminal Underworlds : Looking Down on Society from Below". Kelly, Robert J. ed.: *Organized crime : Cross-cultural studies*. Totowa, NJ, Rowman & Littlefield. 10–31

Kerner, H.-J. 1973. *Professionelles und organisiertes Verbrechen : Versuch einer Bestandsaufnahme und Bericht über neuere Entwicklungstendenzen in der Bundesrepublik Deutschland und in den Niederlanden*. Wiesbaden, Bundeskriminalamt

Kinzig, J. 2004. *Die rechtliche Bewältigung von Erscheinungsformen organisierter Kriminalität*. Berlin, Duncker & Humblot

Kleemans, E.R. & H. van de Bunt 2002. "The social embeddedness of organized crime". *Transnational Organized Crime* 5, 1. 19–36

Kleemans, E.R. & C. de Poot 2008. "Criminal Careers in Organized Crime and Social Opportunity Structure". *European Journal of Criminology* 5,1. 69–98

Klerks, P. 2003. "The network paradigm applied to criminal organisations : theoretical nitpicking or a relevant doctrine for investigators? Recent developments in the Netherlands" Edwards, A & P. Gill eds.: *Transnational Organized Crime : Perspectives on Global Security.* London, Routledge. 97–113

Knoke, D. & J.H. Kuklinski 1982. *Network Analysis.* Newbury Park, Sage

Köbben, A.-C. 2002. "The Wallen project". Fijnaut, C. ed.: *The administrative approach to (organized) crime in Amsterdam.* Amsterdam, City of Amsterdam. 73–95

Korsell, L., A, Heber, B. Sund & D. Vesterhav, 2005. *Narkotikabrottslighetens organisationsmönster.* Stockholm, Brottsförebyggande rådet

Kukhianidze, A., A. Kupatadze & R. Gotsiridze 2004. *Smuggling Through Abkhazia and Tskhinvali Region of Georgia.* Tbilisi : TraCCC Georgia Office

Lampe, K. von 1999. *Organized Crime : Begriff und Theorie organisierter Kriminalität in den USA.* Frankfurt am Main, Peter Lang, Frankfurter Kriminalwissenschaftliche Studien 67

Lampe, K. von 2001. "Not a Process of Enlightenment : The Conceptual History of Organized Crime in Germany and the United States of America". *Forum on Crime and Society* 1, 2. 99–116

Lampe, K. von 2002. "Organized crime research in perspective". Duyne, P.C. van, K. von Lampe & N. Passas eds.: *Upperworld and Underworld in Cross-Border Crime.* Nijmegen, Wolf Legal Publishers. 189–198

Lampe, K. von 2003. "Criminally exploitable ties : a network approach to organized crime". Viano, E.C., J. Magallanes & L. Bridel eds.: *Transnational Organized Crime : Myth Power and Profit.* Durham, NC, Carolina Academic Press. 9–22

Lampe, K. von 2003b. "Organising the nicotine racket : Patterns of criminal cooperation in the cigarette black market in Germany". Duyne, P.C. van, K. von Lampe & J.L. Newell eds.: *Criminal Finances and Organising Crime in Europe.* Nijmegen, Wolf Legal Publishers. 41–65

Lampe, K. von 2004. "Measuring Organized Crime : A Critique of Current Approaches". Duyne, P.C. van, M. Jager, K. von Lampe & J.L. Newell eds.: *Threats and Phantoms of Organized Crime Corruption and Terrorism.* Nijmegen, Wolf Legal Publishers. 85–116

Lampe, K. von 2005a. "Organized Crime in Europe". Philip, R. ed.: *Handbook of Transnational Crime and Justice.* Thousand Oaks, CA, Sage. 403–424

Lampe, K. von 2005b. "Explaining the emergence of the cigarette black market in Germany". Duyne, P.C. van, K. von Lampe, M. van Dijck & J.L. Newell eds.: *The Organized Crime Economy : Managing Crime Markets in Europe.* Nijmegen, Wolf Legal Publishers. 209–229

Lampe, K. von 2005c. *Proposal for a Common European Approach to Assess Organized Crime.* Assessing Organized Crime project, Deliverable 22, 30th November 2005

Lampe, K. von 2006a. "The cigarette black market in Germany and in the United Kingdom". *Journal of Financial Crime* 13, 2. 235–254

Lampe, K. von 2006b. "The Interdisciplinary Dimensions of the Study of Organized Crime". *Trends in Organized Crime* 9, 3. 77–95

Lampe, K. von 2007. "Criminals are not alone : Some observations on the social microcosm of illegal entrepreneurs". Duyne, P.C. van, A. Maljevic, M. van Dijck, K. von Lampe & J. Harvey eds.: *Crime Business and Crime Money in Europe : The Dirty Linen of Illicit Enterprise.* Nijmegen, Wolf Legal Publishers. 131–155

Lampe, K. von, M. van Dijck, R. Hornsby, A. Markina & K. Verpoest 2006. "Organized Crime is...: Findings from a cross-national review of literature". Duyne, P.C. van, A. Maljevic, M. van Dijck, K. von Lampe & J.L. Newell eds.: *The Organisation of Crime for Profit : Conduct, Law and Measurement.* Nijmegen, Wolf Legal Publishers. 17–42

Levi, M. 2003. "Organising and Controlling Payment Card Fraud : Fraudsters and their Operational Environment". *Security Journal* 16, 1. 21–30

Liddick, D. 1998. *The Mob's daily number : organized crime and the numbers gambling industry.* Lanham, MD, University Press of America

Luczak, A. 2004. *Organisierte Kriminalität im internationalen Kontext : Konzeption und Verfahren in England, den Niederlanden und Deutschland.* Freiburg, Edition iuscrim

Lupo, S. 2002. *Die Geschichte der Mafia.* Düsseldorf, Patmos

Mack, J.A. & H.-J. Kerner 1975. *The Crime Industry.* Lanham, MD, Lexington Books

Maljevi, A., D. Datzer, E. Muratbegovi & M. Budimli 2006. *Overtly About Police and Corruption.* Sarajevo, Association of Criminalists in Bosnia and Herzegovina

Maltz, M.D. 1990. *Measuring the Effectiveness of Organized Crime Control Efforts.* Chicago, Office of International Criminal Justice, University of Illinois at Chicago

Markina, A. 2007. "Cigarette black market in Estonia". Duyne, P.C. van, A. Maljevic, M. van Dijck, K. von Lampe & J. Harvey eds.: *Crime business and crime money in Europe : The dirty linen of illicit enterprise.* Nijmegen, Wolf Legal Publishers. 195–208

Massari, M. 2003. "Transnational organized crime between myth and reality : the social construction of a threat". Allum, F. & R. Sieber eds.: *Organized Crime and the Challenge to Democracy*. London, Routledge. 55–69

Matrix Knowledge Group 2007. "The illicit drug trade in the United Kingdom". www.homeoffice.gov.uk/rds. London, Home Office

McAndrew, D. 2000. "The structural analysis of criminal networks". Canter, D. & L. Alison eds.: *The social psychology of crime : groups, teams and networks*. Aldershot, Ashgate. 51–94

McClean, D. 2007. *Transnational Organized Crime : A Commentary on the United Nations Convention and its Protocols*. Oxford, Oxford University Press

McIllwain, J.S. 2001. "An equal opportunity employer : Opium smuggling networks in and around San Diego during the early twentieth century". *Transnational Organized Crime* 4, 2. 31–54

McIllwain, J.S. 2004. *Organizing Crime in Chinatown : Race and Racketeering in New York City, 1890–1910*. Jefferson, NC, McFarland

Merton, R.K. 1957. *Social Theory and Social Structure*, Revised and Enlarged Edition. New York, The Free Press

Moore, W.H. 1974. *The Kefauver Committee and the politics of crime 1950–1952*. Columbia, MI, University of Missouri Press

Morselli, C. & C. Giguere 2006. "Legitimate strengths in criminal networks". *Crime, Law and Social Change* 45, 3. 185–200

Morselli, C. & P. Tremblay 2004. "Criminal achievement offender networks and the benefits of low self-control". *Criminology* 42, 3. 773–804

Natarajan, M. 2000. "Understanding the structure of a drug trafficking organization : A conversational analysis". Natarajan, M. & M. Hough eds.: *Illegal Drug Markets: From Research to Prevention Policy*. Monsey, NY, Criminal Justice Press. 273–298

Natarajan, M. 2006. "Understanding the Structure of a Large Heroin Distribution Network : A Quantitative Analysis of Qualitative Data". *Journal of Quantitative Criminology* 22, 2. 171–192

Naylor, R.T. 2003. "Towards a General Theory of Profit-Driven Crimes". *British Journal of Criminology* 43, 1. 81–101

Newell, J.L. 2006. "Organized crime and corruption : the case of the Sicilian mafia". Duyne, P.C. van, A. Maljevic, M. van Dijck, K. von Lampe & J.L. Newell eds.: *The Organisation of Crime for Profit : Conduct, Law and Measurement*. Nijmegen, Wolf Legal Publishers. 147–175

Obradovic, V. 2004. *Trafficking in women in Bosnia and Herzegovina*. Sarajevo, The Embassy of the United States of America

O'Kane, J.M. 1992. *The Crooked Ladder : Gangsters Ethnicity and the American Dream*, New Brunswick, NJ, Transaction

Pace, D.F. & Styles, J.C. 1975. *Organized Crime: Concepts and Control*. Englewood Cliffs, NJ, Prentice Hall

Paoli, L. 1995. "The Banco Ambrosiano case : An investigation into the underestimation of the relations between organized and economic crime". *Crime, Law and Social Change* 23, 4. 345–365

Paoli, L. 2003a. "The 'invisible hand of the market' : the illegal drugs trade in Germany, Italy, and Russia". Duyne, P.C. van, K. von Lampe & J.L. Newell eds.: *Criminal Finances and Organising Crime in Europe*. Nijmegen, Wolf Legal Publishers. 20–43

Paoli, L. 2003b. *Mafia Brotherhoods : Organized Crime, Italian Style*. New York, Oxford University Press

Paoli, L. & C. Fijnaut 2006. "Organized crime and its control policies". *European Journal of Crime, Criminal Law and Criminal Justice* 14, 3. 307–327

Paoli, L. & P. Reuter 2008. "Drug Trafficking and Ethnic Minorities in Western Europe". *European Journal of Criminology 5*, 1. 13–37

Passas, N. 1999. *Informal value transfer systems and criminal organizations : A study into so-called underground banking networks.* The Hague, Research and Documentation Centre Ministry of Justice

Pearson, G. & Dick Hobbs 2001. *Middle market drug distribution.* London: Home Office

Potter, G.W. 1994. *Criminal organizations: vice racketeering and politics in an American city.* Prospect Heights, IL, Waveland Press

Potter, G. & L. Gaines 1995. "Organizing crime in Copperhead County' : an ethnographic look at rural crime networks". Albanese, J.S. ed.: *Contemporary Issues in Organized Crime.* Monsey, NY, Criminal Justice Press. 61–86

Pütter, N. 1998. *Der OK-Komplex : Organisierte Kriminalität und ihre Folgen für die Polizei in Deutschland.* Münster, Verlag Westfälisches Dampfboot

Rebscher, E. & W. Vahlenkamp 1988. *Organisierte Kriminalität in der Bundesrepublik Deutschland : Bestandsaufnahme Entwicklungstendenzen und Bekämpfung aus Sicht der Polizeipraxis.* Wiesbaden, Bundeskriminalamt

Reuter, P. 1983. *Disorganized crime: The economics of the visible hand.* Cambridge, MA, MIT Press

Reuter, P. & J. Haaga 1989. *The Organization of High-Level Drug Markets : An Exploratory Study.* Santa Monica, Rand Corporation

Robins, G., J. Koskinen & P. Pattison 2008. "Missing data in social networks : Model-based inference". Berlin, Paper presented at the 7th Blankensee Colloquium "Human Capital and Social Capital in Criminal Networks"

Roth, J. 2005. *Aneta M. : Gejagt von der Polenmafia*. Frankfurt am Main, Eichborn

Ruggiero, V. 2000. *Crime and Markets : Essays in Anti-criminology*, Oxford, Oxford University Press

Ruggiero, V. & K. Khan 2007. "The Organisation of Drug Supply : South Asian Criminal Enterprise in the UK". *Asian Journal of Criminology* 2, 2. 163–177

Ruggiero, V., N. South & Eurodrugs 1995. *Drug use markets and trafficking in Europe*. London, UCL Press

Savona, E.U., C. Lewis & B. Vettori eds. 2005. *EUSTOC : Developing an EU Statistical apparatus for measuring Organized Crime, assessing its risk and evaluating organized crime policies, Final Report*. Trento, Transcrime

Segell, G.M. 2007. "Reform and Transformation : The UK's Serious Organized Crime Agency". *International Journal of Intelligence and CounterIntelligence* 20, 2. 217–239

Sieber, U. & M. Bögel 1993. *Logistik der Organisierten Kriminalität*. Wiesbaden, Bundeskriminalamt

Siebert, R. 2007. "Mafia Women : The Affirmation of a Female Pseudo-Subject : The Case of the 'Ndrangheta'". Fiandaca, G. ed.: *Women and the Mafia : Female Roles in Organized Crime Structures*. New York, Springer. 19–45

Smith, D.C. 1975. *The Mafia Mystique*. New York, Basic Books

Smith, D.C. 1991. "Wickersham to Sutherland to Katzenbach : evolving an 'official' definition for organized crime". *Crime, Law and Social Change* 16, 2. 135–154

Smith, D.C. 1994. "Illicit Enterprise : An Organized Crime Paradigm for the Nineties". Kelly, R.J., K.-L.Chin & R. Schatzberg eds.: *Handbook of Organized Crime in the United States*. Westport, CT, Greenwood. 121–150

Southerland, M. & G.W. Potter 1993. "Applying Organization Theory to Organized Crime". *Journal of Contemporary Criminal Justice* 9, 3. 251–267

Sparrow, M. K. 1991. "The application of network analysis to criminal intelligence : An assessment of the prospects". *Social Networks* 13, 3. 251–274

Spencer, J., K. Aromaa, M. Junninen, A. Markina, J. Saar & T. Viljanen 2006. "Organized crime corruption and the movement of people across borders in the new enlarged EU : A case study of Estonia Finland and the UK : Interim Project Report". *HEUNI Paper* 24. Helsinki, HEUNI

Standing, A. 2006. *Organised crime : A study from the Cape Flats*. Pretoria, Institute for Security Studies

Suendorf, U. 2001. *Geldwäsche : Eine kriminologische Untersuchung*. Neuwied, Luchterhand

Sund, B., G. Ahrne, L. Korsell, F. Augustsson, A. Heber, L. Källman, S. Elwér, K. Wallström & J. Skinnari 2006. *Häleri : Den organiserade brottslighetens möte med den legala marknaden*. Rapport 6. Stockholm, Brottsförebyggande radet

Surtees, R. 2008. "Traffickers and Trafficking in Southern and Eastern Europe : Considering the Other Side of Human Trafficking". *European Journal of Criminology* 5, 1. 39–68

Thrasher, F.M. 1927. *The Gang : A study of 1313 Gangs in Chicago*. Chicago, University of Chicago Press

Tremblay, P., B. Talon & D. Hurley 2001. "Body Switching and Related Adaptations in the Resale of Stolen Vehicles : Script Elaborations and Aggregate Crime Learning Curves". *British Journal of Criminology* 41, 4. 561–579

United Nations 2007. *2007 World Drug Report*. New York, United Nations

Vander Beken, T. 2004. "Risky-business: a risk-based methodology to measure organized crime". *Crime, Law and Social Change* 41(5) [pp 471–516]

Vander Beken, T. & Defruytier, M. 2004. "Measure for Measure: methodological tools for assessing the risk of organized crime". P. C. van Duyne, M. Jager, K von Lampe & J.L. Newell (eds.), *Threats and Phantoms of Organized Crime Corruption and Terrorism*, Nijmegen: Wolf Legal Publishers [pp 51–84]

Vander Beken, T., Savona, E.U., Korsell, L.E., Defruytier, M., Di Nicola, A., Heber, A., Bucquoye, A., Dormaels, A., Curtol, F., Fumarulo, S., Gibson, S. & Zoffi, P. 2004. *Measuring Organized Crime in Europe : A feasibility study of a risk-based methodology across the European Union*. Antwerp-Apeldoorn: Maklu

Varese, F. 2001. *The Russian Mafia: Private protection in a new market economy*, Oxford, UK: Oxford University Press

Varese, F. 2004. "Mafia Transplantation". J. Kornai, B. Rothstein, S. Rose-Ackerman (eds.). *Creating Social Trust in Post-Socialist Transition*. New York: Palgrave Macmillan [pp 148–166]

Varese, F. 2006. "How Mafias Migrate: The Case of the 'Ndrangheta in Northern Italy". *Law & Society Review* 40(2) [pp 411–444]

Verfaillie, K. & Vander Beken, T 2008. "Interesting times: European criminal markets in 2015". *Future* 40(5) [pp. 438–450]

Vettori, B. 2006a. *Tough on Criminal Wealth: Exploring the Practice of Proceeds from Criminal Confiscation in the EU*, Dordrecht, The Netherlands: Springer

Vettori, B. 2006b. "Comparing data sources on organised crime across the EU : A first step towards an EU statistical apparatus". P.C. Duyne, A. Maljevic, M. van Dijck, K. von Lampe & J.L. Newell (eds.). *The Organisation of Crime for Profit: Conduct, Law and Measurement*, Nijmegen, Wolf Legal Publishers [pp 43–67]

Volkov, V. 2000. "The Political Economy of Protection Rackets in the Past and the Present". *Social Research* 67(3) [pp 709–744]

Warren, J. F. 2003. A Tale of Two Centuries : The Globalisation of Maritime Raiding and Piracy in Southeast Asia at the end of the Eighteenth and Twentieth Centuries, Singapore: National University of Singapore, Asia Research Institute, Working Paper Series No. 2

Weitzer, R. 2007. "The Social Construction of Sex Trafficking: Ideology and Institutionalization of a Moral Crusade". *Politics & Society* 35(3) [pp 447–475]

Weschke, E. & Heine-Heiß, K. 1990. *Organisierte Kriminalität als Netzstrukturkriminalität Teil 1*, Berlin: Fachhochschule für Verwaltung und Rechtspflege

Williams, P. & Godson, R. 2002. "Anticipating organized and transnational crime". *Crime, Law & Social Change* 37(4) [pp 311–355]

Woodiwiss, M. 1990. *Organized crime USA : changing perceptions from Prohibition to the present day*. Brighton, UK: British Association for American Studies, BAAS Pamphlets in American Studies 19

Woodiwiss, M. 2003. "Transnational organized crime: the global reach of an American concept". A. Edwards & P. Gill (eds.), *Transnational Organized Crime : Perspectives on global security*, London: Routledge [pp 13–27]

World Economic Forum 2005. The Global Competitiveness Report 2005–2006, Geneva: *World Economic Forum*

Wright, A. 2006. *Organized Crime*. Cullompton, Devon: Willan Publishing

Zaitch, D. 2002. Trafficking Cocaine: Colombian Drug Entrepreneurs in the Netherlands, The Hague: Kluwer Law International